THE
CRUThin

A History of the Ulster
Land and People

First published 1974 by
Pretani Press

This edition published 2014 by
Colourpoint Books
an imprint of Colourpoint Creative Ltd

Colourpoint House, Jubilee Business Park
21 Jubilee Road, Newtownards, BT23 4YH
Tel: 028 9182 6339
Fax: 028 9182 1900
E-mail: info@colourpoint.co.uk
Web: www.colourpoint.co.uk

Updated Edition
First Impression

A catalogue record for this book is available from the British Library.

Designed by April Sky Design, Newtownards
Tel: 028 9182 7195
Web: www.aprilsky.co.uk

Printed by GPS Colour Graphics Ltd, Belfast

ISBN 978-1-78073-066-0

In a poem on the Aithechthuatha (who were the 'subject people' of Ireland under the Gaelic-speaking Feni) preserved by Dubaltch* there is mention of the Thuath Sencheneoil or 'Ancient Kindred' who dwelled on the old plain of the Soghain and "stretched eastward across the Suck". This people were a remnant of the Cruithni, Cruthin or Pretani, whose voice has not been heard for a thousand years.

*Genealogical Tracts 1, 75, edited by T Ua Raithbheartaigh
for the Irish Manuscripts Commission.

For Pretania

CONTENTS

ABOUT THE AUTHOR

D R IAN ADAMSON OBE (www.ianadamson.net/myblog) was born on
28 June 1944 in Bangor, County Down and reared in the nearby village
of Conlig. He reads in 15 languages and has spoken publicly in French,
German, Ulidian (Ulster Gaelic), Ullans (Ulster Scots) and Lakota Sioux
at the Ulster Tower in Thiepval and at Guillemont, France; in Dutch at the
16th (Irish) Memorial at Wijtschate (Wytschaete), Flanders, Belgium; in
Turkish at Gallipoli (Çanakkale) in Turkey; and in Mandarin Chinese at
the Chinese Welfare Centre in Belfast. He was an Ulster Unionist member
of Belfast City Council from 1989, becoming its first Honorary Historian,
until his retirement from active politics in 2011, the year he became High
Sheriff of Belfast. He served as Lord Mayor of Belfast in 1996 and was
awarded the Order of the British Empire by Her Majesty The Queen in
1998 for services to local government. He was an MLA for Belfast East
from 1998 until 2003. He was the personal physician and advisor on history
and culture to Rt Hon Dr Ian Paisley PC, the Lord Bannside (First Minister
of Northern Ireland 2007–08), from 2004 until the latter's death in 2014.

He has a special interest in the long-term unemployed and became the
founder Secretary of Farset Youth and Community Development in 1981.
In 1989, he became founder Chairman of the Somme Association based at
Craigavon House, Circular Road, Belfast, under the auspices of Her Royal
Highness Princess Alice Duchess of Gloucester and established the Somme
Heritage Centre at Conlig in 1994. He founded the Ullans Academy,
followed by the Ulster-Scots Language Society in 1992 and became the
first Rector and founder Chairman of the Ulster-Scots Academy in 1994.
He is a founder member of the Cultural Traditions Group, the Northern
Ireland Community Relations Council and the Ultach Trust, and served as
a member of the Ulster-Scots Agency 2003–12. He is presently President of
the Belfast Civic Trust.

Dr Adamson is a Specialist in Community Child Health (Community Paediatrics) being a member of the Faculty of Community Health and was awarded the fellowship of the Royal Institute of Public Health for his services to the health of young people in 1998. He was also awarded a special commendation by His Royal Highness Prince Charles Prince of Wales. He has a special interest in the Mohawk Indians and holds wisdom-keeper status among the Lakota Sioux nation. He is librarian and serving officer of the Commandery of the Ards, the Venerable Order of St John of Jerusalem and a member of the Court of the University of Ulster. He has published several books on the ancient British people known as Cruthin whom he feels should be respected as the primary ancestors of the people of the British Isles. He is a partner in Pretani Associates (www.pretani.co.uk), consultants in Common Identity, founded by Helen Brooker in 2012.

ACKNOWLEDGEMENTS

SINCERE THANKS ARE DUE to Jill Thompson who typed the manuscript, to Isabel Beegle who designed the original maps and to Anne Johnston for the cartography; to Earl, Kevin and Ryan Beegle; David and Rosaleen Adamson; Andy and Agnes Tyrie; Edmund and Kathleen Irvine, and their families; Herbie and Joyce Irvine; David and Linda Campbell; Michael Hall; Wesley Hutchinson; Tom Paulin; Robert and Mark Williamson; Jackie Hewitt and the management committee, staff and students of the Farset Youth and Community Development Limited; Carol Walker, the trustees and staff, former and present, of the Somme Association; the Directors of the Ullans Academy; and all of my family, friends, associates, and indeed opponents, for their support, criticism and encouragement. I would also like to thank the publishers Malcolm and Wesley Johnston of Colourpoint Creative Limited, my editor *par excellence* Rachel Irwin and Jacky Hawkes. Finally I am especially grateful to my friend and colleague in Pretani Associates Helen Brooker, her husband David, and my wife Kerry, without whom I could not have brought *The Cruthin* back into the public domain.

FOREWORD

W HEN I FIRST BEGAN to write books on Ulster history in the late
1960s, it was in an attempt to fill the obvious vacuum which
existed in general public awareness concerning the real roots of the people
of Northern Ireland. The increasing violence and depressing communal
tragedy which continued over two decades and which I witnessed first
hand as a Registrar in Paediatrics in the Ulster and City Hospitals and
the Royal Belfast Hospital for Sick Children only highlighted the need to
make available to Ulster's divided community some very pertinent facts
about their unseen, but very real, shared history and heritage. Little did
I realise then that my own work would itself become part of the debate,
gaining acceptance from all sections of the community, but at the same
time coming under attack from those whose stereotyped views of Irish
history were seriously disturbed by what was being revealed.

One of the main claims made against me was that I was "indulging in
pure revisionism". "Revisionism", as the word implies, means to 'revise'
one's interpretation of history, though often the word is also used in a
pejorative sense, implying that the revision is deliberately undertaken to
help substantiate the revisionist's own particular 'slant' on our past. When
The Cruthin was published 40 years ago in 1974, such a charge of revisionism
might have seemed to contain some validity. After all, terms and concepts
such as 'the Cruthin people', 'the non-Celtic Irish' and 'the Galloway
connection' appeared at that time to be confined mostly to my own work.
Indeed, Michael Hall's summation of my writings in *Ulster – The Hidden
History* must have seemed so unfamiliar to the reviewer in the Linen Hall
Review, that the latter concluded that the historical thesis being expounded
aimed "at nothing less than an overthrow of current perceptions".

To introduce something apparently so 'new' into the historical debate
might, therefore, have served to confirm the 'revisionist' label. Yet before
we come to such a conclusion, let us consider the following quotes:

"In the north [of Ireland] the people were Cruithni, or Picts ... If the [Uí Néill] failed to subdue the south thoroughly, they succeeded in crushing the Ultonians, and driving them ultimately into the south-eastern corner of the province. They plundered and burned Emain Macha, the ancient seat of the kings of the Ultonians, and made 'sword land' of a large part of the kingdom ... Consequent on the [Uí Néill] invasion of Ulster [was] an emigration of Irish Cruithin or Picts [to Scotland] ... The men of the present Galloway were part of the tribe known in Ireland as Cruithni, that is Picts, and only differed from the Picts of [Scotland], in having come into Galloway from Ireland."

To readers aware of the present controversy these quotes might appear to be a reasonable précis of some of my own writings. In fact, I am not the author of the quotes: they have been taken from the ninth edition of the *Encyclopaedia Britannica*, published between 1876 and 1886 – over 130 years ago. My father bought me this encyclopaedia from Claney's Auction Rooms in Bangor when I was eight years old and I read it from cover to cover over the next few years. The *Britannica's* historical interpretation was not an isolated one, however – many books of the period took a similar approach. With his deep interest in archaeology, Edward Carson orientated towards the 'Pictish' origins of the British people, while, as an 'Ulster Scot', James Craig wrote about Dalriada ... As a little boy my father had also bought for me *The Pictish Nation, its people and its Church* by Archibald B Scott, published in September 1918 by TN Foulis of Edinburgh and London, Boston, Australasia, Cape Colony and Toronto. It was printed in Scotland by R & R Clarke Limited of Edinburgh. The author dedicated his book to his father and mother, and to the memory of his youngest brother who died, in 1916, of wounds inflicted in action and sleeps in France with other comrades of the 1st Cameron Highlanders. This wonderful book was my introduction to the Picts.

Richard Hayward was my favourite author at this time, so as my prize for being First in History in Bangor Grammar School Lower Fourth (First Form), at the age of 12, I chose his *In Praise of Ulster*, first published by Arthur Barker of London in 1938 and illustrated by J Humbert Craig. In this volume we read:

"At the time of which we speak the four Southern kingdoms, including that of the Ardri were Celtic in character but it is not certain that the Ulster Kingdom was Celtic; it seems more likely that Ulster was made up of a more ancient Irish people than the Celts, who were comparative newcomers. They seem to have been known as the Cruithni, but we will call them the Ulstermen, for that is what they were, and it is highly probable that they were descended from the aboriginal pre-Celtic Irish people, with some possible connection to the old Pictish race. It is quite certain anyway that these Ulstermen considered themselves different from the Southern Irish even in that yesteryear, and in the face of present-day controversy it is piquant to think that they most likely looked upon themselves as the real Irish people and upon the Southern invaders as a motley crew of foreign Celtic interlopers!"

Richard continued this theme in *Ulster and the City of Belfast* (1950) and *Border Foray* (1957) published by Arthur Barker, with illustrations by my old friend Raymond Piper.

While I have clarified and amended such historical interpretations, having taken into consideration more recent archaeological and historical conclusions, the direction of my enquiry was in fundamentally the same vein. Yet in the second half of the twentieth century there occurred a definite change in emphasis. The Irish somehow came to be considered as most definitely Celts, and references to pre-Celtic population groups such as the Cruthin were unaccountably deleted from most history publications. Even the present (dare I say 'revised') edition of the *Britannica*, in its section on Irish history, no longer makes mention of the Cruthin or even the 'Galloway connection'. Indeed, when we look closely at much of the academic material brought out over this period, it would appear that extensive 'revision' has indeed taken place, a revision which played down these former pre-Celtic and British aspects. It is ironic, then, that if the charge of revisionism can be substantiated, it is not with relation to *The Cruthin*, but to what has been taking place since the middle of the last century among the urban elite, who have indulged in a process of selective historical awareness. Yet, when we come to look at what has been written by a few eminent academics in the past few years, a remarkable – and for some, no doubt, uncomfortable – about-face seems to be occurring. Increasingly, historical evaluation is returning to some of that earlier thinking, with many previous misinterpretations having been corrected, of course – and it is the more-recent history that has been found 'wanting'.

It has also been said that some Loyalists have tried to use my work in their efforts to justify a sectarian position, in the hope that it might give a new credibility to the idea of a 'Protestant Ascendancy', only this time in cultural terms – a 'we were here first' mentality. How a proper reading of my work could lead to the supposition that the descendants of the Cruthin are somehow now exclusively Ulster Protestants is hard to fathom. Actually many individuals within the Protestant section of the community, including the Dalaradia organisation, are showing great interest in the common identity theme I have promoted for so many years and are not only feeling a new confidence in their own identity, but have a desire to share this British Isles (Pretania) identity with the Catholic section of the community. In many ways a cultural battle is now on, in which interpretations of history are right to the forefront. It is a battle in which narrow and exclusive interpretations, which served to consolidate each section of the community's supposed hegemony of righteousness, are under attack from a much broader and inclusive interpretation of all the facets which go to make up our identity. A positive outcome of this battle might just help to drag the people of Northern Ireland away from their obsessions with distorted history and the divisive attitudes of the past. It is in this spirit that we offer this revised 40th anniversary edition of *The Cruthin* to the general public once again.

Dr Ian Adamson OBE
1 July 2014

PROLOGUE

I N THE SECOND CENTURY AD there came from upper Egypt one of the greatest of Ancient Scientists, at once a mathematician, astronomer and geographer. His name was Claudius Ptolemaeus – and we know him as Ptolemy the Greek. Ptolemy wrote for us the *Almagest* where he refers to Ireland as Mikra Brettania (Little Britain), in contrast to the larger island, which he called Megale Brettania (Great Britain). Later he wrote the *Geographike Hyphegesis*, a magnificent work in eight books, and from the account he gives of Ireland, we have the oldest documentary evidence that exists of this island. The account is a remarkable one, for the proportion of tribal and geographical names which can be identified with names occurring in Gaelic literature is very small – only one in four – while a large proportion of names in Great Britain noted by Ptolemy have survived to modern times, even though the Celtic speech has long since disappeared from the greater part of that island. Thus of the 15 river names in Ptolemy's Ireland, only two can be traced in Gaelic records, though of some 50 river names he gives us of Great Britain, about one half have survived to the present day. This is all the more astonishing when we consider the accuracy of Ptolemy's knowledge of Great Britain and it brings into dispute the whole mass of Gaelic Genealogical literature which would tell us that the Gaels have inhabited Ireland from time immemorial, and which even today contrary to the most advanced Celtic Studies, maintains the opinion that the Gaels are the 'native Irish'.

In the early centuries of the Christian era the ethnic origins of the different sections of the Irish population were vividly remembered, for the great wars between them were still in progress. (These wars are now presented in Gaelic history books as dynastic struggles, which is incorrect). In order to remove from the popular memory the ancient distinctions, and to provide the Gaels with the proper pedigree, at once removing the fact that they were foreign invaders from Spain, and at the same time providing the Irish population generally with a common descent, the Gaelic pseudo-historians boldly taught that their ancestors, the sons of Mil, had arrived in Ireland some 2000 years before they actually did. Fortunately these medieval scholars did not succeed in obliterating the traditions of the people themselves, which tell a different story. And the story and traditions which were not destroyed were those of the most ancient inhabitants of Britain and Ireland to whom a definite name can be given. These people were the Cruthin of Ulster, who emerge so distinctively from the pages of the *Life of St Columba* (*Vita S Columbae*) written by Adomnán, who was ninth Abbot of Iona and lived from about AD 624 to 704. It is my purpose to trace these people to the present time and to give them back the history which has been denied them for so long, for they are the Ancient Kindred of Ireland as well as Britain. In doing so I hope that their origins will provide for them a basis of common identity rather than the cause of that running sore which is 'The War in Ireland'.

1 January 1974
BELFAST

CHAPTER 1

THE ANCIENT KINDRED AND THE ERAINN

The word 'Celtic' is primarily a linguistic term which is applied to a closely related group of Indo-European dialects. This family of dialects is usually divided into two sub-groups, 'Q-Celtic' which retained the original Indo-European 'q' and 'P-Celtic' which modified this to 'p'. From the Q-Celtic parent developed Gaelic (Irish, Scottish and Manx) and from the P-Celtic parent Gaulish and Brittonic, now represented by Welsh, Cornish and Breton. 'Celtic' has also been used to describe the so-called La Tène cultural period of the second Iron Age in Western Europe (500–50 BC), and on the evidence of historians, be equally applied to certain tribes whose names are known. But the term may not be used to denote ethnic origins any more than 'English' may.

In the following thesis Adomnán's distinctive 'People of the Cruthin' (Cruthini populi) may be traced both to highlight the unalterable ethnic affiliations of the people of Northern Ireland and Britain, and at the same time to deny Celtic racialism and the Gaelic hegemony in Ireland. Such essentially linguistic terms as 'Gaelic' and 'Brittonic' are used of peoples of a common country and way of life with the proviso that such usage has serious limitations. These should become apparent as the story unfolds. The usage, however, is broadly excused by the little known fact that the 'Gaels' and 'Britons', although possessed of very similar forms of society, literature and law, and in supposed frequent contact with each other, never knew that they had a common 'Celtic' origin and considered themselves in Medieval Times as absolutely distinct peoples. This is in remarkable contrast to the Anglo-Saxons, who, although never so bombastic about their origins, always retained the known links with the Old Saxons of Germany.

There is little doubt that even in the centuries before Christ the 'Celtic' Tribes were composed of different physical types, and that Celtic speech was adopted by or imposed upon large numbers of subjects. The true 'Celtic' homeland has been said to have lain in Central Europe. Whether this is right or not remains to be seen, but there was certainly a core area of Celtic-speaking people in south-western Gaul itself, from where they then spread to the Atlantic coast, Iberia, Italy and beyond. If one defines a specific 'Celtic' type there, anthropometric and genetic surveys of the peoples of Northern Ireland and indeed of Ireland show that such types account for a small proportion only of the present population. Much more common are older population groups classified as Atlanto-Mediterranean, Neolithic and especially Upper Palaeolithic in type. Such studies, of course, cannot indicate when these peoples arrived and still less what language or languages they spoke in the Elder Days. Suffice to say, however, in Ballymena, County Antrim, which was settled most completely by Scottish immigrants in the seventeenth and eighteenth centuries, 60% of the population belong to these three ancient types alone. Indeed one modern genetic study indicates that the percentages of the present population whose ancestry precedes c 4,000 BC are 88 per cent of the Irish, 81 per cent of the Welsh, 79 per cent of the Cornish, 70 per cent of the Scots and 68 per cent of the English. However more DNA evidence is needed from the ancient remains of our ancestors themselves.

But now let us begin again at the beginning. We have no evidence of human habitation in Ireland before the retreat of the ice-sheets which covered almost the whole of the island until the end of the Ice Age. The first settlers came about 7000 BC in the period known as the Mesolithic or Middle Stone Age. One of the attractions which the North of Ireland offered Mesolithic Man was the abundance of flint in the chalk outcrops of the Antrim Coast. These flint-users were hunters, fishermen and food-gatherers who lived predominantly along the coast or in river valleys such as the Bann. Shortly after 4000 BC, during the Neolithic or Late Stone Age, farming was introduced. Crops were grown, animals kept and many new types of implement were introduced. For the first time our ancestors began to leave their mark on the thickly wooded Irish countryside. The tombs and monuments made by these Neolithic Farmers were 'Megalithic', ie made of large stones, eg the court cairn and dolmen. The burial ritual normally employed was cremation and alongside the cremated remains were placed 'grave-goods', pottery, flint and stone implements, and weapons – which reveal a good deal of information about the Neolithic way of life.

The introduction of metallurgy into Ireland is generally ascribed to those artisans who also made a type of pottery to which the name 'Beaker' has been given. Three objects found near Conlig, County Down include a copper knife or dagger of Beaker type, a small copper axe of early type and a small copper dagger of more advanced type. The mines of Conlig are still extant and the area was probably the main source of copper ore in the North. The working of bronze commenced in Ireland around 1800 BC. In the beginning the ancient Irish bronze smiths provided the needs of much of Britain, and to a lesser extent of northern and western Europe as well. Later technical developments followed similar courses throughout the British Isles and influences from abroad became more apparent. The most important of these were from the Iberian Peninsula, and trade between these two places must have been brisk. The outstanding problem remains that such a great bronze industry should be carried out on an island where tin, which accounts for some 10% of the alloy, was not mined to any degree. This tin must have come from Cornwall, Brittany or even north Spain. For such importing to be carried out there must have been a highly sophisticated civilisation, which runs contrary to the general notion of an uncivilised people existing before the 'Celts'.

About 1200 BC there was a change in the type of the implements, and a whole new variety appears, distinctive of what we know as the late Bronze Age: there were torques of twisted gold, gorgets of sheet gold and loops of gold with expanded ends used as dress fasteners. This was indeed a Golden Age for Ireland, peaceful and prosperous, controlled by a society in which craftsmen were even more in evidence than warriors, and open to the trading influence of the Mediterranean. It lasted until the third and second centuries BC, when the use of iron implements superseded the use of bronze to a greater or lesser extent. The bronze of three swords of this era found at Ballycroghan near Bangor proves on spectroscopic analysis to contain a fair proportion of lead (about 10%) as well as copper and tin. As the tin is present in the correct proportion for a good quality alloy (9–10%), it is apparent that the lead has not been used as a cheap substitute for the expensive imported tin, but is more likely to have come from the copper used. This is in keeping with copper ores found at Conlig, among which the crystalline masses of Galena (Lead Sulphide) can be seen, and with which the early Cruthin must have been familiar. It remains for us to study the trading influences at work in the Mediterranean at that time.

The advancement of the ancient peoples of these times in the science of navigation has been very much under-rated, for the first attempt of Jason and his Argonauts to Colchis (modern Georgia) has led to the erroneous conclusion that before that period nautical skill was very low, and shipbuilding confined to small craft. While the Greeks themselves were in a comparative state of barbarism, Phoenician mariners had explored not only the Mediterranean, but the Atlantic, beyond the Pillars of Hercules at Gibraltar to the coasts of Spain, France and the British Isles, and the northern coasts of Africa, were well acquainted with the Indian Ocean, and sent in their seasons commercial fleets to all these parts with all the regularity of a mercantile nation. With exception of the lack of acquaintance with the magnetic compass, they appear to have been equal to the accomplishment of most voyages achieved in modern times.

Phoenicia was the ancient name of a very small country situated between the 34th and 36th degrees of north latitude on the Eastern Mediterranean coast to the north of Palestine. The northern boundary is stated by Ptolemy to be the River Eleutherus and Pliny, Mela and Stephanus place it rather more northward in the island of Aradus, but the confines of the republic must have varied at different times. On the coast were numerous cities – the most famous were Tyre and Sidon. The climate of that place was agreeable and salubrious, and the soil fertile and productive, so that this Land of Lebanon was a prosperous and pleasant land.

But consider the words of the Prophet Ezekiel in his 27th chapter of the Book of God, written about 500 BC, when the Tyrians had already been trading for centuries:

"Say unto Tyre, O Thou that art situate at the entry of the sea, and carry on merchandise with the people of many isles, thus saith the Lord God, O Tyre, thou has said, 'I am of perfect beauty.' Thy borders are in the midst of the seas; thy builders have perfected thy beauty. They have made all thy shipboards of fir trees of Senir, and have taken cedar trees of Lebanon to make thy masts. Of the oaks of Bashan have they made thine oars; the company of Azurites have made thine hatches of well worked ivory, brought out of Chittim. It was of fine linen and Phrygian broidered work from Egypt which thou madest thy spreading sails; and thy covering was of the blue and purple of the isles of Elishas. The Sidonians and the men of Arvad were mariners in thy service, and wise men thy Pilots, O Tyre were in thee. The elders of Gabel, and their able workmen were those who caulked the seams of thy vessels, and all the ships of the sea were employed in carrying thy merchandise ... The merchants of Tarshish traded at thy fairs on account of the great variety of all kind of thy riches, and brought silver, iron, tin and lead to thy market ... The ships of Tarshish did sing in praise of thy commerce, and thou wert replenished and made glorious in every part of the ocean. Thy rowers brought thee into great waters; the east wind hath broken thee in the midst of the seas ... What city is like Tyre, like the destroyed in the midst of the sea? When thy waves went forth out of the seas, thou fillest many peoples; thou didst enrich the kings of the earth with the multitude of thy riches and they merchandise".

Where Ezekiel speaks of the rich purple dyes from the Isles of Elishas we may have the first written reference to the British Isles. The purple dyes of our Islands were celebrated among the later Greeks and Romans, and were very expensive. But his Isles of Elishas may have been nearer home.

These words of Ezekiel were of a Phoenicia in decline, but they show the magnificence of the great ships which plied between Tarshish and Tyre in Olden Times. Traditionally Tarshish has been connected with the region of Tartessos in southern Spain, which is known principally from a sixth century Greek logbook *The Massiliote Periplus* (*Ora Maritima* of Festus Avienus), and thought to be in the Guadalquivir valley. But Tarshish stood also for all the lands of the far west with which the Phoenicians traded, for it was the collecting point for produce from West Africa, tin from the mines of north-west Spain, or the richer deposits of Cornwall, as well as the rich mines of silver and other metals to which the navigable rivers of Guadiana and Guadalquivir gave easy access. The tin islands (Cassiterides) were reached from Brittany, and are always distinguished from the British mainland. Strabo dates the settlements west of the straits of Gibraltar soon after the time of Tyre's first expansion which we know from the travelogue of the Egyptian Den-Amir, written about 1070 BC, was already in progress.

It was the special trade with Tarshish which made the commercial greatness of the Phoenicians, and led to their colonisation of Spain and the

West African coast. This explains why the latter settlements are related to the earliest phase of Tyrian and Sidonian expansion in the early centuries of the first millennium BC. Thus the farthest points were settled first, and the need for intermediate stations to secure connection was felt later. Josephus has fortunately preserved for us extracts from two Hellenistic historians, Dius and Menander of Ephesus, which supply us with a synopsis of the history of the Golden Age of Tyre. Thus we learn that Hiram I, son of Abibal, reigned from 980 to 946 BC and was the great friend of Solomon, King of the Jews. The relations between Jews and Phoenicians had been generally friendly before this; it appears from Judges 5:17, Genesis 49:13 & 20, that Asher, Zebulon, and Dan acknowledged some dependence on Sidon and had in return a share in its commerce.

The two nations grew closer under the Kings. Hiram built David's palace (2 Samuel 5:11), and also gave Solomon cedar and fir trees from Lebanon, as well as workmen for his palace and temple, receiving in exchange large annual payments of oil and wine. With similar commercial interests it was only natural that the two kings should send joint expeditions to King Solomon's Mines on the coast of Aqaba at Ophir, and to the British Isles via Tarshish. What were the names of the two great islands by which they knew them? Our earliest sources are Greek so that we don't really know, but the Latin author Festus Avienus writing about the year AD 380 (*Ora Maritima*, 'Sea Coasts') mentions the voyage of Himilco the Phoenician to Ireland in the year 510 BC. Himilco is said to have called our island the Holy Island (Sacra in Latin), its inhabitants to have been mariners navigating in hide-covered barks the Irish Sea. That these people were not 'Celts' we can see in their matrilineal form of inheritance, the polyandrous nature of their society and their original non-Indo-European speech, which survived latest in Caledonia. The *Periplus of Himilco* is a description of a Phoenician expedition through the coasts of western Europe which took place at the same time as the circumnavigation of Africa by Hanno (c 500 BC). *Ora Maritima* includes references to the islands of Ierne and Albion, Ireland and Britain, whose inhabitants traded with the Oestrymnides of Brittany. Sacra in Greek would have been hieros, perhaps a scribal confusion with Ierne.

We know that Tartessos had been trading with the Greeks since the voyage of Colaeus beyond the Pillars of Hercules about 638 BC. On the site of present day Marseilles in southern France, the enterprising Greek mariners of Phocaea in Asia Minor founded about 600 BC the Colony of Massalia (in Latin Massilia). This settlement of Greeks in waters which the Phoenicians and their children the Carthaginians jealously reserved for their own commerce was not effected without a naval conflict. It is, indeed, not improbable that the Phoenicians were settled at Marseilles before the Greek period, and that the very name of the place is Phoenician. The great fall of the Ionic cities before the Persians, however, cut off the remote city of Massalia from close connection with the mother country. Isolated amidst alien populations, the Massaliots made their way by the greatest prudence in dealing with the inland tribes, by the vigilant administration of their oligarchical government, and by frugality and temperance united to remarkable commercial and naval enterprise. Their colonies spread east and west along the coast from Monaco to Cape St Martin in Spain, carrying with them the worship of Artemis. The Carthaginians, on the other hand, worshipped Baal Hammon and his female counterpart Tanit. The name of the famous Carthaginian general Hannibal means 'he who enjoys Baal's favour'.

Massalia was situate in the country of the Ligurians, an early non-Celtic people, later engulfed by the extension of the 'Celtic' realm. The main trading routes of the Massaliote Greeks reached up the Rhône and Saône to the Swiss Lakes and the upper Danube, where culture was in the late 'Hallstatt' phase, ie in the mid-sixth century BC. It was thus from the 'Celts' that the earliest Greek historians derived the scant knowledge they possessed of the British Isles. And very scant was the information that the 'Celts' were able to give at a time when there existed a people who imported tin to Ireland from Cornwall and north Spain, so well were the coastlines known. Let us first state that the name 'Celt' was never applied to the peoples of Britain and Ireland so far as is known, and there is no evidence that the natives ever used this name of themselves. By native, I mean those people, the ancient kindred, who traded with the Phoenicians. The Great Greek philosopher Aristotle, who lived in the early fourth century BC, wrote of a large island called Ierne which lay "beyond the Celts", and stated that it was discovered by the Phoenicians, the name in whose language would have meant 'the uttermost habitation'. The sister island was known as Albion. These names had come to the general knowledge of Greek geographers such as Erathosthenes by the middle of the third century BC. Together they were known to the Greeks via their allies the Celts as the Pretanic Islands or Islands of the Pretani (Pretanikai nesoi), which may possibly be from the Phoenician Bratanac, or Barat-anac (Country of Tin) or more probably an indigenous name which the people used for themselves. About 50 BC the Greek Diodorus wrote about "those of the Pretani who inhabit the Country called Iris (Ireland)". It is the identification which these people make among themselves which remains important to one and shows that they were a different people from the 'Celtic' Britons and Gaels.

It has long been recognised that Pretani is the Gallo-Brittonic equivalent of the name which in Old Gaelic is Cruthin, representing the still older 'Q-Celtic' Qreteni. The Gaelic equivalent enables us to identify the Cruthin or Pretani with a large part at least of the people who are now commonly called the Picts. The name Pict in itself, however, as a name of a people of Britain, is found for the first time in a Latin document of AD 297, the panegyric of the future Emperor Constantius. The Welsh form Goidel ffichti also comes from Latin, and at a relatively late time through literature. These were the last of the Irish Cruthin who left Ireland under Gaelic pressure and who, by early Christian times must themselves have spoken Gaelic under their dominance. The original language of the Cruthin was non-Indo-European in all probability, and as we would expect. In Scotland, the language of cultural dominance in early Christian times was P-Celtic, and a form of this was later spoken by the Picts (Caledonian Cruthin). While the *Annals of Ulster* and Adomnán do not apply the name Cruthin to the Picts, the *Pictish Chronicle*, *St Berchan*, the *Albanic Duan*, the *Book of Deer* and John of Fordun plainly show that the names are interchangeable. Also, Tighernach, the ablest and earliest of the Annalists frequently gives the name Cruthin to the Picts of Old Caledonia.

From the early part of the fifth century BC the south-eastern region of Britain received from northern France and the Low Countries a new group of traders. The influence of bearers of an Iron Age culture spread over the course of two centuries as far the Pennines but there is no evidence that they ever reached Ireland. On the continent that reorganisation of wealth and power which gave rise to the La Tène art styles was in progress, although it was not until the middle part of the third century BC that it expressed itself in Britain as the Iron Age B culture. The last phase of actual colonisation of Britain before the Roman Conquest comes with the Belgic settlements in the south-east, during the first century BC. These Belgic colonies gave rise, according to Julius Caesar, to the different petty states of Britain, the name of those from which they came. Caesar's report is the first and only record from historical sources of 'Celtic' or part-Celtic migration to Britain. His evidence is corroborated by the list of British tribes given by subsequent writers in which the Hedui of Somersetshire, the Morini of Dorset, the Senones of Hampshire, the Rheni of Berkshire and Surrey, the Attrebates stretching from the former county into Hampshire, the Cimbri of the borders of Devon, the Parisii on the eastern coast of the island, all had their representatives in Gaul (France).

Since the Belgic settlements of Britain were derived in some part at least from Roman expansion we should briefly note the main points of that expansion and the peoples involved. The final existence of many of these peoples as independent entities will be seen later in Ireland. About 400 BC the Gauls had invaded Italy and sacked Rome. The district in which they settled became known as Cisalpine Gaul and this was conquered by the Romans about 225 BC. By the end of the following century the shadow of the power of Rome fell on the area of Southern Gaul lying between the Mediterranean and the Cevennes. It was the magnificent Julius Caesar however who was responsible for the final extinction of Gaulish independence in his campaigns of 58–51 BC. Caesar's famous 'Gallic Wars' give us a personal account of Gaul of his day which was divided into three parts, inhabited by three nations – Belgae, Celtae and Acquitani, all of whom differed in language, institutions and laws. Since the Romans knew all three as Gauls, and the leaders and tribes, at least, have Celtic names, we may assume all became Celtic-speaking, although of differing dialects and ethnic origins. In general we may say that the Celtae were true 'Celts', the Belgae had strong Germanic elements and may even have spoken a German dialect, and the Acquitani contained strong elements of non-Indo-European stock.

Caesar limits the Celtae to that country included from north to south between the Seine and the Garonne, and from the Ocean on the West to the Rhine in Helvetia, and the Rhone on the east. The Veneti were the most powerful of the Celtae, and inhabited the country to the north of the mouth of the Loire (Liger). There is little doubt that these were the Iron

Age B 'Celts' who landed in south-west England from Brittany. We know that the Domnonii of Cornwall and Devon were the most cultivated of these 'Britons' and that the Veneti traded with their Domnonian brothers for the tin of Cornwall. The Domnonian Britons preserved the legend that they came from Gwas-gwyn and were Lloegrians, ie from the country of the Liger. They also called themselves Lagin in Ireland and from their ancestor deity were Children of Loegaire, or we would say 'Loegairians' from Armorica. Finally when the Irish Lagin invaded the Lleyn Peninsula it took the name of Guined, which derives directly from Veneti.

The Belgae inhabited north-eastern France and the Low Countries. The most important Belgic tribe we have not yet named were the Menapii, who were seated on the Meuse and on the lower Rhine. This great tribe was to become known to the Gaels as the Fir Manaig (Men of the Manapii) who gave their name to Fermanagh and Taughmonagh in Belfast. The Fermanagh we will meet later when they join the Cruthin. It is probable also that they inhabited the Isle of Man (= Manapia) before the Gaelic conquest. It was the Menapii along with the Morini and other northern tribes who maintained an independent Gaulish area following Caesar's campaign of 57 BC. In 56 BC the Veneti threw off the yoke of Rome and the whole coasts from the Loire to the Rhine joined the insurrection. Caesar attacked the powerful Venetian navy and destroyed it, selling the defeated captives into slavery to a man, and it was the help they received from their Brittonic relatives which prompted his invasion of Britain. Since some would have us believe that these peoples knew little of the Atlantic Ocean, let us record Caesar's testimony in toto, so we may assess their migratory capacity:

"The ships of the Gauls (Veneti) were thus built and equipped. Their keels were flatter than those of the Romans, and therefore better calculated for a shallow and flat coast; the forecastle was erect and perpendicular, and the poop was so contrived as to bear the force of the large tempestuous waves. They were altogether built for strength. The ribs and beams were made of a timber a foot square, and fastened with iron belts an inch thick. Instead of cables, their anchors were made fast with iron chains; they also made their sails of hides, either for want, or ignorance of the use of linen for that purpose, or because sails made of linen would scarcely be strong enough to serve ships of so great a burthen, or be able to sustain the force and violence of the tempestuous winds of these seas. The Roman vessels exceeded those ships in the celerity of their motions, by means of their oars, but, in navigating those coasts, and encountering foul weather, they were altogether inferior. They were built so strong that the Romans could not injure them by running their prow or beak heads against them, nor could they throw their weapons with any effect into them, they were of such great altitude, besides which in case of foul weather, these ships could with safety put to sea, or more safely be on a flat shore without fear of the damages to which the sharply built Roman vessels were always exposed."

It is clear from Caesar that Britain prior to his invasion was inhabited by two different peoples, native and colonist. His account of their distinct geographical distribution is not based on his own or on Roman observation, for he and his forces did not penetrate to any part of the island outside of the zone of Belgic colonisation. His statement is based on a long standing tradition of the 'Celts' themselves. Modern archaeology represents a division of Britain before the Romans into two zones, the 'Highland Zone' and the 'Lowland Zone' lying mainly to the north-west and to the south-east respectively, of a line down between Devonshire and the middle of Yorkshire, the Highland Zone retaining in the mass a population less changed by invading elements. In the process of 'Celtic' colonisation from over sea there was obviously an early stage in which the colonists were disturbed along the seaboard, leaving the older population relatively undisturbed in the interior regions.

The greatest confusion in the early history of our Islands has been caused by the wrongful acceptance that the name Pretani or Pritani is the same as Brittones or Brittani – the Celtic-speaking Britons. Julius Caesar's 'Britons' were in the main descendants of the Celtic invaders, Belgic and non-Belgic, who do not appear to have had a common name for themselves until they adopted it from the Latin. It does not seem feasible that the Romans mistook the name Brittones for Pretani, for they were very scrupulous in adopting the names of native tribes into Latin. Rather it would be more probable that the name Briton derived in Gaul itself and was transcribed accurately by the Romans, although to them all the inhabitants, being barbarians, would eventually be lumped together as 'Britons'. The descendants of the speech of the 'Celtic' Britons are Welsh (= Anglo-Saxon Wealh from Old German Wolah for Celt or Volcae), Cornish and Breton of France. In early Welsh literature Ynys Prydein invariably means the Island of Great Britain and the literal translation of this is the Island of the Pretani (Picts). Otherwise Prydein means Pictland proper (Modern Scotland) or Pretania, the 6,000 British Isles. Thus the very Celtic-speaking Britons themselves respected the ancient possession of Great Britain as Cruthinic and not Brittonic. Now let us look at Ireland, part of the 'Highland Zone' and inhabited, according to the sources used by Diodorus, by "those of the Pretani".

The most ancient Irish traditions specifically state that the Cruthin were the first people of Ireland. This is confirmed by the *Pictish Chronicle* which states that "Thirty Kings of the Cruthin named Bruide" ruled Ireland and Scotland. Then came the Builg, commonly known as the Fir Bolg, and these we can easily identify with the Belgae. This again is confirmed by tradition which states they were Britons and their invasion legend tells how their ancestor Lugaid came from Britain to conquer Ireland. Following these Britons, the names of whose tribes we see in Ptolemy's geography of Ireland, came a group of tribes which included the Galioin, the Domnonains, and the Lagin. The Lagin held on to and gave their name to Leinster. According to their own invasion legend they were in origin Gauls who invaded Ireland from Armorica. Latest of all came the Gaels from Spain, speaking an archaic Q-Celtic, as distinct from the P-Celtic of the preceding tribes. By the time of the oldest period of Irish Prose, AD 650 to 750, as exemplified by manuscript Laud 610, the Gaels and Erainn (Belgae) had been made congeners from Mil (The Soldier) of Spain. Laud 610 describes how the Milesians, under Cormac, son of Art, son of Conn of the Hundred Battles, won the sovereignty of Ireland by a decisive victory over the Cruthin at Fochairt. "By force" the story does "did they gain the sovereignty of Ireland, and by force they hold it always". By the end of the eighth century the Cruthin themselves were made into Gaels, and in the *Lebor Gabála Érenn* there is a virtual denial of the existence of a permanent Cruthinic element in the population of Ireland at any time.

The *Lebor Gabála Érenn* is a medieval scholarly attempt to give 'Gaelic' ancestry to all the peoples of Ireland at that age, while maintaining the older origin legends. The title given to the composition may be translated

'The Book of the Taking of Ireland' and in the redactions of early history and tradition which have come down to us we can trace not a little of the true history of our country. According to the *Lebor Gabála* the first invasion after the Biblical Deluge was by Parthalon. The name Parthalon is not Gaelic, and it is reasonable to suppose that this so-called invasion is a learned invention which had displaced the earlier traditions that the Cruthin were the first people of Ireland.

The next invasions of Ireland according to the pseudo-historical scheme are of the greatest value. These concern the invasion of Nemed's People, and also the Fir Bolg or Belgae, a substantial part of whom were actually Erainn or Iverni. Nemed is also stated to have been the ancestor of the Britons. The story is told of how a son of Nemed called Fergus sailed from Ireland with his son Britan from whom all the Britons who inhabited Great Britain were descended. Thus it was admitted by the pseudo-historians that the Children of Nemed were of the same kin as the Britons. We know of course that the Britons inhabited Great Britain before they invaded Ireland, and not vice versa. There exists a convention in the Gaelic pseudo-history books of turning the invaders into exiled Irishmen returning with victorious armies or explaining kinship by the successful invasion from and not to Ireland. Thus the ancestor of the Erainn, Lugaid, is said to have led an army from Britain and conquered Ireland, but only following Lugaid's wrongful banishment for Ireland. The banishment has been added as the standard cover-up story to the genuine traditions of the Belgic Erainn, that they came to Ireland from Britain where they had already acquired power. Despite the teachings of the genealogists the non-Gaelic origin of the Erainn was long remembered. The Fir Bolg tribes are all represented in Ptolemy's geography, while on the other hand there is not a trace of any Gaelic tribal name. The Iverni of Ptolemy were situated in what is now County Cork, the name having survived as Erainn. They are recorded in early historical times as the Corcu Loigde of Western Cork, the Corcu Duibne of Kerry, The Corcu Baiscinn of West Clare, the Calraige of Sligo and the Desi of East Munster.

Yet the most important remnants of the Belgae were the Dál Riata of North Antrim and the Dál Fiatach of North Down and Ards (The Darini of Ptolemy). These two tribes formed with the Cruthin an Ulster Confederacy dominated by the Dál Fiatach, which was to challenge the central Gaelic power for a thousand years, and the descendants of the two peoples are the Ulster Scots. The ancient legend of the battle of Crinna would suggest that at the time of the Gaelic invasion of Ireland the supremacy of the 'Ulaid' existed as far south as the Boyne River, and that the Gaels had no opponents north of that river apart from the Ulaid. Thus the name of the Ulaid was used as a comprehensive designation for tribes of both Cruthinic and Belgic stock. Through the Kings of the Dál Riata are all the Kings and Queens of Scotland descended, and through this line is descended the present Queen of the British Peoples. Her most ancient possession is that of Ulster. It is also of note to record that Fergus, the great Pictish Lord of Galloway, who ruled the last remnant of the Irish Cruthin was also an ancestor of the present British Royal Family. Of the last of the Cruthin of Ulster we shall see more later. Let us first return to the Invasions of Ireland and consider them from the archaeological point of view.

The early phase of the use of iron implements in Ireland extended over about the last two centuries BC and a little beyond. It is marked by the appearance in north-east Ireland of such equipment as iron swords and their bronze scabbards made and ornamented in a version of La Tène, which is based on continental rather than British models. This is consistent with the growing isolation from Britain apparent at the end of the late Bronze Age. Implements of Late Bronze Age type continued to be a marked feature and burial customs persisted from the Earlier Age. Excavation of Downpatrick at least showed that life continued unbroken. None of this is evidence of a 'Celtic' migration to Ireland, rather it shows that an ancient land of craftsmen was learning new ways. If there was a movement from the Continent it could only have been of Chieftains and their retinues or of craftsmen alone. We may tentatively delineate this period, however, as the beginning of 'Celtic' influence in Ireland.

Since the Belgic invasion of Britain is an occurrence which both history and archaeology agree in placing in the early part of the first century BC, and the whole of Irish tradition assuages the fact that the Fir Bolg were the people who controlled most of Ireland before the coming of the Gaels, we must of necessity place the Belgic invasion of Ireland at a later date. Archaeology indeed places the main Brittonic settlements in Ireland during the first century AD. Until this time contacts between the Iron Age peoples of Britain and the people of Ireland do not seem much indicated by natural remains. There may be occasional relationships in matters of ornament and contacts between important individuals across the Irish Sea, but virtually no objects of distinctly Brittonic type in the first phase have been found in Ireland. During the first century AD, however, objects characteristic of the Britons appeared in the eastern parts of Ireland. Population movements are confirmed by consulting Ptolemy's map where we find the Iverni (who knew themselves as the Fir Bolg or Belgae) living in Munster proximally to the Belgic tribes of South Britain, while the Ulster Voluntii (Uluti or Ulaid) are placed proximally to a large tribe of that name living in present-day Lancashire. The name Fir Bolg would probably have become the common name for Britons of non-Belgic as well as Belgic stock, so we cannot give a precise date for the first Brittonic settlements in Ireland. To this day, however, there is no evidence which can place them in Ireland before the first century AD or the first century BC at the earliest. The nature of any settlement, if there were any before this time, remains pure conjecture. Subject to cultural influences before this time, Ireland, undoubtedly was, but the established myth of the 'Ancient Gael' belongs in the Irish context to the Celtic Twilight World of the Patriot Poets and the Gaelic nationalist academic elite.

The next historical invasion of Ireland in the Medieval Scheme was by the Lagin, who gave their name to Leinster. The Lagin preserved the tradition that 'Lagin', 'Domnainn' and 'Galioin' were three names for the one people, and this is in direct conflict with the nationalist teaching of the pseudo-historians and the genealogists. According to this teaching the Galioin and the Domnainn were among the pre-Gaelic invaders of Ireland, whereas the Lagin were Gaels. Thus the names Galioin and Domnainn dropped out of use as being of a second-class people, and only the name Lagin were conceded honourable. Either this or the Galioin and Domnainn were exterminated completely by the Gaels. There is little doubt that these people were a branch of Ptolemy's Dumnonii of Devon and Cornwall. Ptolemy also placed Dumnonii or Damnonii around Dunbarton, and they seem to have extended southwards into Renfrew, Larnark and Ayr. If, as seems very likely, they are another branch of the Lagin, it would seem probable that they reached Dumbarton due to early Roman pressure on the south. The Irish Laginian invasion legend tells us how their ancestor (Labraid Loingsech) led a force from Armorica to Ireland, and this invasion

31

either took place via Cornwall and Devon or directly from Gaul. This people conquered a considerable part of the present provinces of Leinster and Connacht, but made almost no impression on Ulster and Munster. What happened to them following this partial conquest? Well, most of them appear to have entered the service of the Invader Gael. The Gaels rewarded them with 'Sword Land' in return for tribute and mercenary service. Foremost among these mercenary tribes were the Galioin under the name of Gailing. However, whatever may have been the mercenary relationship of the Leinstermen to the Gaels, they retained enough of their ancient heritage to consider themselves a distinct people until Medieval Times. It is essential to realise this in any study of Irish History. The Domnainn of Connacht whom we meet in the Ulster Sagas were probably a branch of those Domnonii Ptolemy places in Dumbarton.

The Gaelic invasion of our country was of course the longest and most complete. So total has become the Gaelic dominance in language and culture that even in these Modern Times Gaelic Ireland is synonymous with Irish nationalism, and the Gaelic tongue is unequivocally known as 'Irish'. That the Irish Gaels suffered under later English domination is but one side of a coin which carries on the obverse the long cruel extermination of the population and culture of the Ancient Kindred of the Ulster People. The claim of the Gael to Ireland is by the sword only, and by the sword was it reclaimed in later days by the descendants of those Ancient Peoples – namely the Belgic Dál Riata and the Cruthin. Of these two Ulster Peoples the paramount claim belongs to the Cruthin, last of the Picts. The list of pre-Christian kings of Ireland found in the *Lebor Gabála* is for the most a pure fabrication to provide the Gaels with the correct pedigree as rulers of Ireland from time immemorial. By what amounts to a conspiracy of silence broken only by a sponsored mythology of half-truths and religio-political emotionalism, the Gaelic pseudo-historians still rule. What remains unpardonable is the lack of progressive education and research on the subject, which is the duty bounden on our universities and schools. For traditional, historical and linguistic considerations all support the conclusion that the Gaelic settlement of Ireland was a LATE event in Irish history.

The genuine traditions relate how Tuathal Techtmar led the ancestors of the Midland Gaels to Meath while Mug Nuadat (Eogan) led the Southern

Gaels to Munster. The enmity which arose between these two groupings led to a division of Ireland arbitrarily into Conn's half and Mug's Half, which has historical significance (Conn was Tuathal's grandson). The creation of the Midland Gaelic Colony, which became known as Mida (Meath), was not effected without continuous warfare. The southern Gaelic invasion seems on the other hand to have been effected fairly peaceably and relations between the Eoganacht (Munster Gaels) and the Erainn (Munster Belgae) were amicable at first. This was not to last.

In the great Gaelic literary masterpiece the *Táin Bó Cúailgne* or *Cattle Raid of Cooley* are embodied the traditions of the ancient Ulster peoples in their struggles against successive invaders, Belgic and Gaelic. The specific text tells of a War between the 'Ulaid' and the 'Connachta' and the events are traditionally dated to the first century of the Christian Era. Among the chief dependants of the 'Connachta' in the Saga is Ferdiad mac Damain of the fighting Gamanraid (Domnonians). It would therefore appear that the main traditions enshrined in the Ulster Sagas are (1) the early warfare between the Domnonians and Belgae of the West and the Cruthin and (2) the later warfare between the descendants of Conn (Connachta), aided by their dependants, against the Ulaid. By the middle of the seventh century AD, when the Táin took literary form, the West was known as Connacht and memories of the Gallo-Brittonic ways of war were mingled with more recent political realities. The great hero of the *Ulster Cycle of Tales* was Cú Chulainn, whose real name was Setanta, which is cognate with a tribe of Britons who lived in Lancashire. Setanta is specifically stated not to have been of the Ulaid, and the borders he patrolled so well reached, as we have previously stated, as far south as the Boyne River. This would seem to have been the furthermost southern limit of the power of the Darini, as merely a warrior aristocracy, while the bulk of the northern population were Cruthin, who claimed to be the real Ulaid (Uluti, Usluntii or Voluntii). The Belgae derived from Britain and, since population movements in Europe around the time of Christ were due, directly or indirectly, to the expansion of Rome, let us return to and relate the main events of the Roman Invasion of Britain. For it was as a consequence of Roman pressure that Brittonic tribes were driven to the north and west of that island, and the Brittonic settlements of Ireland were most likely to have been effected.

CHAPTER 2

THE ROMANS

IN THE LATE AUTUMN of 55 BC Caius Julius Caesar invaded the mainland of Britain, landing at some point along the south-eastern coast. He returned the following year to defeat a Confederation of Brittonic Tribes under Cassivellaunus. Caesar's expedition to Britain was looked upon as one of the military triumphs of the age. The Roman People honoured with enthusiasm the great commander who had led their favourite legions into a new world (penitus toto divisos orbe Britannos, 'deeply divided from the whole world are the British') and who had forced all the south-eastern tribes, from the Iceni or Cenimagni of Suffolk to the inhabitants of Hampshire, to acknowledge the supremacy of Rome. During the reigns of Augustus and Tiberius, which together make up a period of nearly 80 years, these Britons were left in a position of friendship and alliance with the Roman Empire. The power wielded by Cassivellaunus seems to have descended to Tasciovarus, father of the famous Cymbeline.

Cymbeline was a powerful and distinguished prince, as we can see in the numerous coins he executed. Yet during the later years of his reign such rivalry arose between his three sons, Adminius, Caractacus and Togodumnos, that he was forced to exile Adminius to Gaul. Adminius, however, went straight to Rome to claim the protection of the Emperor Caligula. Caligula marched an army to the Gaulish coast with the threat of reducing Britain to a province, and restoring Adminius. True to his nature Caligula then ordered the Roman soldiers to gather shells from the beach, and led them back to Rome with the 'spoils of the ocean'. Mercifully for humanity Caligula was assassinated in AD 41 by his own Praetorian Guards.

Civil war was however to continue in Britain between the sons of Cymbeline and the sons of another British Belgic Prince named Commius. One of the latter called by Dio Cassius, Bericus or Vericus, fled from Britain to the court of the new Emperor, the noble Claudius, explaining to him the condition of Britain and how it would easily be conquered. And so, in the year AD 43, a Roman Army under the able command of Aulus Plautius landed on the shores of our sister island. He was met in battle first by Caractacus and then by his brother Togodumnus, and these brothers he defeated in turn. In pursuing them he overran the whole south of 'England' as far as Oxfordshire and Gloucestershire, the country of the Dobuni. This people were at the time under the dominion of the Catuellani, the hereditary tribe of the great Cassivellaunus, and probably of Cymbeline. Among the distinguished soldiers who led the Romans were Vespasian and his son Titus, both of whom were destined to become Emperors of Rome. It was therefore among the Britons that those soldiers were trained which destroyed that Jerusalem where Jesus was crucified. Of the Wars of the Jews one can read in the *Works of Josephus*.

Meanwhile the Sons of Cymbeline having retreated before Plautius towards the west, seem then to have doubled back on their Roman pursuers and sought refuge in the marshy lands of the lower part of Essex. Here it was that Togodumnus was killed at length by the Romans. The death of Togodumnus caused such anger among the Britons that Plautius soon found himself of the defensive, and was forced to send to reinforcements from the Continent. Claudius himself then landed in Britain to command his legions. Under his inspiration the Romans again crossed the Thames and decisively defeated the south-eastern Britons. Claudius returned to Rome in triumph, and both he and his son were honoured by the Senate with the title of Britannicus.

The Roman legions now turned their attention to the south-east, where, extending from Hampshire to the extremity of Cornwall, lived the powerful tribes the Belgae proper and the Domnonii. After a long and obstinate struggle with the second Legion under Vespasian (who we are told by Suetonius fought nearly 30 battles and captured 20 Brittonic fortified positions), the south-west submitted to the Romans. Until this period material contacts between Ireland and Iron Age peoples of Britain are not indicated to any extent by modern archaeology. Virtually no objects of distinctly British type in the first phase have been found in Ireland. This is in full accord with Irish tradition that the Fir Bolg or Belgae were the Brittonic invaders of Ireland. The pattern of Brittonic material remains becoming prominent in the first century AD also relates to Southern

Scotland, although the later part of this may be due to a planned Roman policy of population movement, and not to refugees.

Prior to the year AD 50, Aulus Plautius was recalled, leaving his legions still at war with the Britons. He was succeeded by a capable new governor by name Ostorius Scapula. Ostorius was greeted with an invasion of the Roman Province by inland tribes, on whom he inflicted such a counter attack that they were repulsed with great slaughter. Ostorius proceeded to build a line of forts (castra or 'chesters') from the Avon River to the Severn. Thus, voluntarily, or by compulsion, all the tribes from the farthest coast of Norfolk to the Land's End had submitted to the authority of Rome. Of those who submitted voluntarily the most important were the Iceni, who lived in that area demarcated by the modern counties of Suffolk, Norfolk, Cambridge and Huntingdon. Jealous of the line of forts which Ostorius had built, the Iceni rebelled and following their defeat, the submission of the Provincial tribes was complete. Beyond the new boundary of Roman Britannia lay the great Brittonic tribe of the Brigantes, who extended through the mountainous and wooded districts from the borders of Lincolnshire, through Yorkshire, Lancashire, Cumberland and Westmorland (modern Cumbria) and Northumberland. Lesser tribes, such as the Cornavii and Coritavi lay between the Romans and the Brigantes. Ptolemy also places the Brigantes in South Wexford, and they survived unto the period of documentary history as the Uí Bairrche, giving their name to the Barony of Bargy in South Wexford. It is probable that the Brigantes invaded Ireland under pressure from the later Belgic and Gaulish (Domnonian) tribes, and that prior to this they had lived in parts of Britain more proximal to Wexford. Only when the waves of Celtic migration reached the fastness of northern Scotland did they finally lose their force.

The defeat of the Iceni had a sobering effect on the Brigantes, who appear to have then paid tribute to the Romans. Ostorius however had reached the territory of the Gangani in North Wales when he had to return to quell a revolt by dissidents among the Brigantes. The Gangani also lived in the west of Ireland and were probably a tribe of Commius. Only the Silures were then left to carry on the struggle against Ostorius. This tribe had rallied under Caractacus the defeated son of Cymbeline, and under his leadership entered into a confederacy with the Ordovices of North Wales. Ostorius's victory against the confederation was a decisive one, and Caractacus, who had fled to the Brigantes, was delivered up to him by the Brigantian Queen, Cartismandua. The dignity with which Caractacus and his family faced the court in Rome is related by the historian Tacitus. Following the capture of their Prince, the Silures commenced a guerrilla war against the Roman occupation, which so wore down the fine conventional soldier Ostorius that he died.

Civil war then broke out among the Brigantes, the one faction under the Queen, Cartismandua, supporting the Romans, while her husband Venusius commanded the opposite faction, who were strengthened by the Silures and other tribes. The rebel faction was again defeated, but disorder continued among both Brigantes and Silures. The Roman legions were now being led by the able commander Caius Suetonius Paullinus who, while destroying the centre of Druidic worship at Mona (Anglesea), was called back urgently to deal with a dangerous revolt by the Iceni. The Iceni had been kept in obedience only by fear, and their king, Prasatagus, had hoarded great wealth during the reign of Nero, when corruption was rife among the imperial officers of government. Hoping to secure protection for his wife and family, he died leaving half his riches to the Emperor, and the other half to his two daughters. He was no sooner buried than the Roman officers took possession of his kingdom, and when his Queen Boadicea (Boudicca) resisted, publicly scourged her. Then the Iceni rose, and were soon joined by the Trinobantes of Essex. Camulodunum (Colchester) fell to the insurgents and the Ninth Legion under Cerealis was then destroyed. Suetonius returned quickly from Anglesey, but was forced to sacrifice first London and then Verulamium to his enemies. He then however crushed utterly the Icenian people and Boadicea, unwilling to survive the destruction of her country, committed an honourable suicide.

Following the destruction of the Iceni there appears to have been a temporary change in policy towards the Britons. Suetonius Paullinus appears to have been a strict and harsh ruler, and his treatment of the conquered people brought him into conflict with the new procurator, Julius Classicianus, who had been sent as the successor of the decadent Catius Decianus. An imperial agent, Polycletus, was despatched from Rome to inquire on the state of the Province, and it was probably his report that led to the recall of Suetonius. He was succeeded by the Consul Petronius Turpilianus, and under the lenient rule of this man many of the wounds of the previous years were healed. Petronius resigned shortly before the death of Nero, but was fortunately followed by Trebellius Maximus who governed the province with equal moderation. Thus, while the rest of the Empire was torn by civil strife following Nero's death, Roman Britannia enjoyed an unusual peace. This was disturbed, however, by a quarrel which arose between the governor and Roscius Coelius, lieutenant of the twentieth legion. As the soldiers generally took the side of Coelius, Trebellius was forced to leave Britain and joined the standard of Vitellius. Vitellius had already drawn from the Province a body of 8,000 troops, while Suetonius had carried over the whole of the fourteenth legion to fight under the standard of Otto.

When Vitellius won the throne, therefore, he sent the fourteenth legion to Britain with one of his trusted attendants, Vettius Bolanus. Tacitus tells us that the government of Bolanus "was too mild for so fierce a province, and Agricola, who was still serving in Britain, checked the ardour of his own martial disposition in case he should be suspected of disobedience or disaffection towards his commander-in-chief." The security of the province was endangered by the new struggle for the Empire between Vitellius and Vespasian, which drew off much needed troops. At this point the Brigantes again revolted. The Romans had continued to maintain the authority of Cartismandua, who in contempt of her husband had taken as her lover his armour-bearer Vellocatus. Venisius raised an army against her, and she was rescued with difficulty by the Romans, who were forced to leave the Brigantes in a state of independence. On the accession of Vespasian, various changes were made in the establishment in Britain. Petilius Cerealis, the commander of the Ninth Legion, who had been defeated in the war against Boadicea, was sent to succeed Vettius Bolanus as governor, while Julius Agricola assumed command of the twentieth Legion. After several successful engagements with the Brigantes, who were for the most part reduced to obedience, Cerealis was recalled and Julius Frontius appointed to his place. Under this governor the Silures were also conquered. In the year AD 78, however, Julius Frontius was recalled, the Ordivices of North Wales destroyed a cavalry troop stationed among them, and the Britons were again ready to rise in general revolt. At this moment there was appointed governor the one main in the Empire capable of keeping Britain Roman, and that was Agricola. Gnaeus Julius Agricola was Governor of Brittania from AD 78–84 in that period known as the Flavian AD 69–96, during the reigns of the three emperors whose family name was Flavius. Agricola was a fine soldier as well as a statesman, and his attempt to define a frontier in North Britain has been fully documented by his son-in-law Tacitus in a biography written about AD 98. Before we summarise the career of Agricola, let us return to Ptolemy and consider Tacitus's concept of Caledonia.

Let us first give a brief resume of the main tribes north of the Brigantes so we may study the political and ethnic groups into which they fell. The Vottadini (Goddodin) occupied the whole coast-district between the southern Tyne and the Firth of Forth, which comprehends the half of Northumberland, the whole of Berwickshire and East Lothian, and the eastern part of Roxburgshire. Their stronghold was Brenenium on Reed-water, in Northumberland. The Gadeni inhabited the interior country immediately west of that of the Vottadini. This comprehended the western part of Northumberland, a small part of Cumberland, the western part of Roxburgh, all Selkirk and Tweeddale, much of the mid-Lothian, and nearly all West Lothian. Curia, on the Gore-water was their chief place.

Now we come to Galloway, which was to become so important in the history of the Ulster-Scottish peoples. The whole of Dumfriesshire, and the eastern part of Galloway as far as the Dee was occupied by the Selgovae, who probably gave their name to the Solway. Their chief places were Trinontium at Brunswark-hill in Annandale, Uxellum at Wardlaw-hill in Caerlaverock and Caebantorigum at Drummore in the parish of Kirkcudbright. The Novantes possessed all central and western Galloway between the Dee and the Irish Sea, and had as their principal towns Lucopibia, on the site of the present Whithorn, and Rerigonium on the northern shores of Loch Ryan. The Damnonii (Domnonii) inhabited all the expanse of country from the mountain ridge which divides Galloway and Ayrshire on the south to the River Earn on the north, comprehending all the shires of Ayr, Renfrew and Stirling, all Strathclyde, and a small part of the shires of Dunbarton and Perth, and had the towns of Vanduaria on the site of Paisley, Colania in the south-eastern extremity of Strathclyde, Coria in Carstairs, Aluana on the River Alan, Lindun near the present Ardoch, and Victoria on Ruchil-water in Comrie. The Albani, who were later subjugated by the Damnonii, inhabited the interior districts between the southern mountain screen of the loch and River Tay, and the mountain chain along the southern limit of Invernesshire comprehending Breadalbane, Athol, Appin, Glenorchy and a small part of Lochaber. There is little doubt that all these tribes were Brittonic, as their subsequent history proves.

Now let us read from Tacitus:

"Whether the inhabitants of Britain were indigenous or foreigners, being barbarians, they (the Romans) did not take the trouble to enquire. The different character of their bodily appearance in different parts of the island gave rise to arguments. The red hair and big limbs of the natives of Caledonia point to a German origin. The coloured faces of the Silures, their hair, generally plaited, and Spain being opposite gave credit to the opinion that the ancient Iberi had migrated and occupied these settlements. Those nearest the Gauls were like them, whether on account of the enduring force of descent, or the position of the sky determining in lands adjoining the character of the races. On a general view it is credible that the Gauls occupied the neighbouring island. You may detect the same sacred rites and superstitions. There is not much difference in their language."

Tacitus described as Caledonia the whole Highland region lying to the north of the line between the Firths of Forth (Boderia) and Clyde (Clota). From the corrected map of Ptolemy that region which was to become the main Pictish area, bounded by the Moray Firth, the Great Glen and the Forth-Clyde line, was inhabited by four tribes, the Caledonii, Taezali, Vacomagi and Venicones. These names are by no means Celtic, and in derivation are probably part of that old Pictish tongue which was spoken by the mass of the Pictish population. Traces of this non-Celtic tongue are found in the historical part of the Pictish King list, and the Pictish Ogham inscriptions are written in it entirely. The Caledonii proper inhabited the whole interior between the mountain range along the north of Perthshire to the Beauly Firth and the traces of their name are still found in such modern place names as Schiehallion and Dunkeld. If Pinnata Castra represents the Roman fort at Inchtuthil at the southern end of Strathmore, then the home of the Vacomagi lay between the Tay and the Dee. The Taezali inhabited the northern part of Kincardineshire and all of Aberdeenshire, while the Venicones lay between the Firths of Forth, and their associated place name Orrea has been identified with the site of a Roman fort at Carpow on the south side of the Tay Estuary. The names given by Ptolemy to the tribes of the west coast and far north are the Epidii of Kintyre, the Creones further north, the Carnonaceae of Western Ross, the Caereni of north-west Sunderland, the Cornavii of Caithness and the Lugi of Sutherland with the Smertae between them and the Decantae of Easter Ross. These names are merely Celtic descriptive terms. There is no reason to believe other than that the population was composed of 'Bronze Age' natives under a more or less Celticised aristocracy, the Celtic spoken having Gaulish antecedents.

So, in the year 78 Agricola, at the age of 38, commenced his famous military career in Britain. In his first campaign he slaughtered nearly the whole tribe of the Ordovices and destroyed the power of Anglesey. The next year he succeeded in reducing and Romanising the Brigantes and in AD 80 carried Roman arms to the Taw (Tay) estuary. In his fourth campaign he overran all the Eastern and central Scottish lowlands to the Forth and Clyde. In his fifth, or in 82, he invaded "that part of Britain which is opposite to Ireland" or lower Nithsdale, and the whole extent of Galloway. Those who would not submit to Agricola became refugees or were exterminated. Thus must the Domnonians have come eventually to Connacht. Tacitus describes this campaign as follows:

"In the fifth campaign, Agricola, crossing over (the Firth of Forth) in the first ship, subdued, by frequent and successful engagements, several nations till then unknown, and stationed troops in that part of Britain which is opposite to Ireland, rather with a view to future advantage, than from any apprehension of danger from that quarter. For the possession of Ireland, situated between Britain and Spain, and lying commodiously to the Gallic sea (Bay of Biscay) would have formed a very beneficial connection between the most powerful parts of the Empire. This island is less than Britain, but larger than those of our sea (the Mediterranean). Its soil, climate, and the names and dispositions of its inhabitants, are little different from those of Britain. Its ports and harbours are better known from the concourse of merchants for the purposes of commerce. Agricola had received into this protection one of its petty kings, who had been expelled by a domestic sedition, and detained him, under the semblance of friendship, till an occasion should offer of making use of him. I have frequently heard him assert that a single legion, and a few auxiliaries, would be sufficient entirely to conquer Ireland, and keep it in subjection, and that such an event would also have contributed to restrain the Britons, by aweing them with the prospect of the Roman arms all round them, and as it were, banishing liberty from their sight".

Thus Agricola and Tacitus knew by commerce enough of Ireland to contemplate its invasion, and it was probably Agricola's staff who wrote those accounts of Ireland and Britain, which were used by Ptolemy. It is a terrible reflection on the mentality of 'Celtic scholars', born of an almost religious reverence for the assumed antiquity of the Gaels of Ireland that they have even tried to prove that the Ireland recorded by Ptolemy was based on sources as early as the fourth century BC. Had the great scholars of the Roman Empire to rely on sources 500 years old for information about an island their soldiers could see every clear day from the coast of Galloway? Yet the renowned Irish linguist TF O'Rahilly could find no evidence of any Gaelic name in Ptolemy's account and those names we can trace of Belgic Brittonic stock. Neither are the Domnonii placed in Ireland. Thus both the Laginian and Domnonian, and then the Gaelic invasions of Ireland must have followed in time Agricola's campaigns.

In the summer of AD 83 Agricola crossed the Forth at what is now called Queensferry, making at this time considerable use of his fleet. His land army, according to Tacitus's theory, advanced in three columns. Almost immediately they encountered vigorous resistance from the tribes in front, while the tribes to their rear commenced to attack the fortifications they had erected for the protection of their conquests. However Agricola pressed forward among the Horestii and found the clans for the first time in mutual co-operation. He was attacked by them at Loch Orr in Fife, but repelled them after a furious engagement. Without much further trouble he brought all the Horestii under his control. In his final campaign in AD 84 Agricola first sent his fleet to harass the Caledonians. His army now included some Britons from the south acting as auxiliaries. It must also be noted that the Roman Army in Britain was composed of many different ethnic groups including many Germans. They advanced from Inchtuthil through Strathmore and Kincardine into Aberdeenshire until their march was barred by the army of the Caledonian Confederacy drawn up on the slopes of Mons Grampians. The battle which ensued was fought near a Roman emplacement, and Tacitus seems to imply that this was the farthest point north which Agricola reached. Tacitus numbers the "strength of all the tribes" who had been assembled for a final stand against the Romans as 30,000 men, and the most outstanding leader was Calgacus "the swordsman". The battle was so obstinate that only night forced it to an end, and the Caledonians retreated at last to the sanctuary of their northern recesses. Apt word indeed does Tacitus give to Calgacus who says of the Romans "For they create a desert and they call it peace".

So, with the Scottish lowlands south of the Lower Tay and the Earn now all in his possession, and a powerful body of the tribes of the conquered district enrolled with him as auxiliaries, a voyage of discovery and of intimidation was ordered by him round the island. In the course of this voyage the Roman fleet subdued the Orcades (the Orkney and Shetland Islands) and saw Thule (Iceland) before returning to the Firth of Forth. Agricola's plan for 'Britannia perdomita' (Britain thoroughly conquered), however, had to be abandoned because he was recalled to Rome through the envy of the Emperor Domitian. Disastrous Roman defeats on the Danube meant the withdrawal of one of Britain's four legions, perhaps as early as AD 86. Because of this the legionary fortress of Inchtuthil (Pinnata Castra) was given up, probably soon after the date of its six latest coins – newly minted Bronze Asses of AD 86. This also involved the evacuation of the Auxiliary Forts to the North and possibly also all the Flavian forts of North Britain, except that at Newstead-on-Tweed. However the silence of history during the 35 years which followed, and absence of any events of interest, shows the power of Agricola's achievements as a general and a statesman. It is probable that during these decades there was a freer movement of new settlers into south-west Scotland. It is also possible that the hill fort on Birrenswark Hill, Dumfriesshire was constructed at this time.

In AD 120, the Emperor Hadrian built his celebrated wall between the Tyne and the Solway, which has acted as an artificial barrier between 'Scotland' and 'England' ever since. Although he did not relinquish the conquered territory north of the wall, he effectually acknowledged himself to hold it by a partial and comparatively insecure tenure. The Vottadini (Goddodin), the Gadeni, the Selgovae and the Novantes began to feel neither overawed nor restrained by the Roman stations which were continued in their territory. Soon they broke out into insurrections and ran southwards in ravaging incursions which the Romans were unable to check. In AD 139, the year after Antonius Pius became Emperor, Lollius Urbicus was created Governor of Brittania. In 140 he marched north to quell what was now a general revolt, and in the following months brought successfully under the power of his arms the whole Lowland country as far as the Beauly Firth. The Campaign is recorded by the late third century writer Capitolinus in his *Life of Antoninus Pius* who he states "conquered the Britons through Lollius Urbicus the governor, and after driving back the barbarians, built another wall, this time of turf". Bronze coins commemorating this victory were minted in late AD 142 or early 143, and thus date the building of the Antonine Wall (from Carriden on the Forth to Dunglass on the Clyde) which immediately followed. The tranquillity of the subjugated tribes, till the death of Antonius in 161, about which time Lollius Urbicus ceased to be governor, sufficiently indicates the vigour of the administration throughout all the Roman territory. Scotland was now divided into three great regions: the district south of Antoninus's wall, which was joined with the Roman government of South Britain; the Lowland country between Antoninus's wall and the Beauly Firth, and which is said to have now been given the provincial title of Vespasiana; and nearly all the Highlands which began to wear more distinctly the name of Caledonia.

Disturbances broke out again immediately on the accession of Marcus Aurelius. These were quickly quelled by Calphurnius Agricola, the successor of Lollius Urbicus, but were followed by a Roman withdrawal of the whole province of Vespasiana. The tribes beyond the wall of Antoninus were thus thrown back into a state of independence. In AD 183 they began to make predatory incursions beyond the wall, which became more regular towards the close of the century, and in 200 made a treaty with the Lieutenant of Severus. Dio Cassius, a contemporary historian, states that the whole country north of the Antonine Wall was held by the Caledonii and the Maeatae, the two "greatest peoples", who had absorbed all the other tribes. The Maeatae, according to Dio, lived close to the wall, and were presumably the inhabitants of Vespasiana, while Caledonii lived beyond them. In 207 the far northern peoples again renewed their hostilities, and provoked Severus to attempt a re-conquest of their territory. Before his Caledonian campaigns Dio says that Severus "bought peace from the Maeatae" and early Severan gold hoards found north of the Forth may be part of the purchasing price. Between AD 209 and 211 Severus reached the extremity of the island (probably the Moray Firth), following much the same routes at Agricola. This is evidenced by the series of large temporary camps in the north-east. Peace terms which were made with the Caledonians were only of short duration, and trouble resumed with both that people and the Maeatae. While Severus died in AD 211 at York, his son Caracalla quickly concluded the Caledonian campaigns. He relinquished to them the territories which they had surrendered to his father, secured to them by treaty independent possession of all the country beyond the wall, and took hostages from them, for the conservation of the international peace.

From this time on for nearly a century the Caledonians ceased to mingle in the Roman story, and the whole island of Britain assumed a political grouping which became relevant to early Christian times. The Caledonians were to become known as Picts, showing that, although Tacitus gave them the overall name of Britons, as inhabitants of the island of Britain, they were actually Pretani or Cruthin. The partially Romanised inhabitants of the region between the Antonine and Hadrian's Walls were to form their own Brittonic States, and according to their own traditions were distinctively Britons, retaining the known ethnic difference between themselves and the Picts. Hadrian's Wall, however, was to remain the frontier of Roman Britannia for the final two centuries of the Roman presence, and only to the south of the wall was Latin, language and culture, the dominant force. Thus far the history of the Caledonian Cruthin. In the next chapter we will return to the Cruthin of Ireland.

CHAPTER 3

THE GAELS

IRELAND WAS KNOWN TO the Romans by the names of Hibernia and Juverna. Ptolemy gives us a description of its coasts and enumerates the tribes and towns both in the maritime districts and the interior. On the northern coast dwelt the Veniconii, in the modern county of Donegal, and the Robogdii in Londonderry and Antrim. Adjoining to the Veniconii, westward, were the Eradii or Erpeditarii, and next to them the Nagnatae, all in Donegal, although the Nagnatae also occupied North Connacht. Further south were the Auteini (the Uaithni) in Sligo and Galway, the Gangani in Mayo, and the Vellabori in the district between the Shannon and Galway. The whole south-west part of the island, with a large part of the interior, was inhabited by the Iverni who were Belgae and probably took their name from the River Iernos or Ivernos which ran through their territory. The name Iernos derives from Ierne or 'Ireland' and has not been proved to be of Celtic derivation, although was obviously used in Celtic speech as 'Ireland' and 'Erin' are used in English. The most obvious explanation is that it is Phoenician for the 'uttermost' or 'farthest' island and passed into Greek.

The south-eastern promontory was known as the 'Holy' Promontory, to the north-west of which, in the modern counties of Waterford and Tipperary, Ptolemy places a tribe called the Usdiae or Vodiae. In the modern county of Wexford dwelled the Brigantes (Uí Bairrche), north of whom were the Coriondi of Wicklow, the Manapii (Fir Manaig), the Cauci on the banks of the Boyne, the Eblani on the bay of Dundalk, the Voluntii or Uluti (Ulaid) in Down, and the Darini (Dál Riata) bordering on the Robogdii in Antrim. Of these tribes we can say with certainty that the Iverni, Brigantes, Manapii, Coriondi, Gangani and Darini were all Brittonic (Fir Bolg), while most of the others must have been Cruthin, especially the Ulster tribes, for it was in Ulster that the Cruthin stood last against the 'Celtic' invaders. Since the Uluti came from Lancashire to Down, and the other Belgic tribes to the east and south-west coasts, the north-western tribes must surely be the Cruthin, the old Pretani. The Veniconii are obviously the same tribe who became known as Picts in Scotland.

The British invasion was to be a Pyrrhic victory for Caesar. In 54 BC Ambiorix brought together an alliance of Belgic tribes, the Eburones, Manapii, Nervii and Atuatuci allied to local German tribes. He launched an attack on 9,000 Roman troops under Sabinus and Cotta, Caesar's favourite generals, at Tongres and wiped them out. Caesar retaliated quickly, determined to exterminate the Belgic confederacy which was ruthlessly ravaged in all-out genocide. Ambiorix, however, was never captured and disappeared from the pages of Continental History, but the Eburones re-emerged in Britain as the Brigantes (Uí Bairrche) just as the Manapii (Managh) came to Ireland.

In 52 BC the brilliant Belgic leader Commius of the Atrebates turned against his former ally Caesar. He led a large force to join the armies of his kinsman Vercingetorix against him in a great insurrection which was to change the course of European history. Following Vercingetorix's defeat, Commius became over-leader of the Belgic Atrebates, Morini, Carnutes, Bituriges, Bellovaci and Eburones, and many Belgae followed him to his British Kingdom in the last 'Celtic' folk movement to Britain, rather than endure the savagery of Roman civilisation. In the 20 years following Julius Caesar's assassination on the Ides of March, 44 BC, Commius' British Kingdom grew in size and wealth. In the nine years from 34 BC there were three occasions under Caesar's successor Octavian (Augustus Caesar), 34, 27 and 26 BC, when a full-scale invasion of Britain was contemplated. Commius then appears to have set up a Belgic enclave around the mouth of the Shannon in western Ireland, which became known as and was recorded by Ptolemy as Gangani, the descendants of Gann, the form of his full Celtic name. Meanwhile his sons took over from one another in surprisingly swift succession as kings of south-east Britain. Each re-emerged as kings of the expanding Belgic settlements in western Ireland; these were Tincommius (Gaelic Sen Gann), Epillus (Eochill) and Verica (Ferach).

By this time the Brigantes controlled the largest section, which is now northern 'England' and a significant part of the midlands, centring on what is now known as Yorkshire. The modern town of York was originally known by the name of Eboracum, founded by the Romans in AD 71 and deriving from the Eburones, whose High Goddess of Sovereignty was Brigantia. Ptolemy also places the Brigantes in South Wexford. Thus they survived into the period of documentary history as the Uí Bairrche, giving their name to the Barony of Bargy. It could be that the Brigantes invaded Ireland under pressure from later Belgic and Gaulish tribes and that prior to this they had lived in parts of Britain which were more proximal to Wexford. But they could also have migrated under pressure from the Romans in the AD 70s. There was also a tribe, of course, known as the Brigantii, whose capital was Brigantion, now Bregenz, on the Lake of Constance, the Bodensee or Swabian Sea (das Schwäbische Meer), known to the ancients as Lacus Brigantinus.

The legendary Ninth Legion, Legio IX Hispana, the Spanish Legion, was one of the oldest and most feared units in the Roman Army. Put together in Spain by Pompey in 65 BC, it came under the command of Julius Caesar when he was Governor of Further Spain in 61 BC. The Legion served in Gaul throughout the Gallic Wars from 58–51 BC, and was decisive in ensuring Caesar's control of the Republic. After Caesar's assassination it remained loyal to his successor Octavian. It fought with distinction against the Cantabrians in Spain from 25–13 BC but suffered terribly in the British revolt led by Boadicea (Boudicca) in AD 60, losing as many as 50–80 per cent of its men. However, several high ranking officers, who could only have served after AD 117, are well known to us, so we can safely assume that the core of the Legion was still extant in the reign of Hadrian, AD 117–138.

The first great leader of the Feni (later 'Gaels') in Ireland, Tuathal (Teuto-valos) Techtmar, was probably a Roman soldier, commanding Q-Celtic speaking auxiliaries from Spain. The earliest known source for the story of Tuathal Techtmar's conquest of Ireland from the Aithech thuatha (Vassal Tribes) is a poem by Mael Mura of Othain (AD 885). Mael Mura intimates that about 750 years had elapsed since Tuathal Techtmar had marched on the ancient British or Cruthin ritual centre of Tara to create his kingdom of Meath, which would date the invasion to the early second century AD. This is probably approximately correct. The standard pseudo-historical convention is employed, however, to make him an exiled Irishman returning with a foreign army. The account in the *Lebor Gabála*

Érenn, is probably older and in this we see that Tuathal was born outside Ireland and had not seen the country before he invaded it. We can thus synchronise his invasion to early in the reign of Hadrian (AD 122–138) and his death fighting the Cruthin near Antrim in the reign of Antoninus Pius (AD 138–161).This fits with Juvenal (AD c 60–127) who wrote "We have taken our arms beyond the shores of Ireland…" Tuathal may therefore represent the fictitious Mil Espáne, or even the Ninth Legion, the Legio IX Hispana, but that we will probably never know.

The information used by Ptolemy we have traced to the period of Agricola's campaigns (around AD 84). Following or during this period the Lagin invaded the modern Leinster area, as we have described, and the Damnonii came from south-western Scotland, under Agricola's own pressure. The struggle for supremacy which ensued, the earliest traditions of which are embodied in Gaelic literary form in the *Táin Bó Cúailgne*, led to the division of Ireland into four parts or provinces. These were the Part of the Iverni (Erainn) now known as Munster, the Part of the Lagin, ie Leinster, the Part of the Uluti (Ulaid), ie Ulster, and Part of Ol Nechnacht, which is now known as Connacht. The Ol Nechnacht are Ptolemy's Nagnatae, the ancient Cruthin of this province who survived as the Cruthin of Cruachain and the Sogain. The population of the area became well mixed with Cruthin, Belgae, then the Domnonian Gamanraid, and finally all these peoples were absorbed by the Connachta (the descendants of Conn, grandson of Tuathal Techtmar) who gave Connacht its final name. With the formation of the Gaelic Midland Colony, Meath, a fifth province was added and this survived to modern times. This no longer officially exists as it has been incorporated into the Province of Leinster. True to the activities of their medieval counterparts the southern historians deem it more appropriate to forget about the Midland Colony and remember only the ancient divisions of Ireland, which better suits the Gaelic Ireland concept.

Considering again the *Ulster Cycle of Tales*, the whole structure of society, the weapons and characteristics of the warriors, and their methods of warfare described agree precisely with the descriptions by classical authors of life among the Britons and Gauls before the Roman invasions. In the case of the Gauls we derive our information from the later Greek historians, Athenaeus, Diodorus Siculus and Strabo, in whose work material from the lost work of Posidonius is reproduced or summarised. The basic political structure described in the Ulster Sagas is that of the old four provinces, and one in which Gaelic nomenclature is an anachronism. Thus the enemies of the Ulaid are known as Connachta at a time when Conn was not even born. From the Táin we learn that the three warrior septs of Ireland were the Gamanraid (Domnainn) from Irrus Domnann, the Clan Dedad of Munster (Erainn), and the Ulaid, all pre-Gaelic tribes.

In the Glenmassan tales the extent of territory occupied by the Domnainn (Domnonians) is portrayed with great minuteness and an abundance of place names, many of which are today unknown, having been erased by the later Gaelic conquests under the Connachta. The descriptions show that they had conquered a stretch of territory which extended from the Donegal-Leitrim boundary to Burren and Loop Head in County Clare, and from Devenish south-west to the sea, that is to say it comprised the present counties of Leitrim, Sligo, Mayo, Galway and Clare. Following their defeat by the Ulaid in the period outlined by the Táin, they are described in *Cath Artig* as losing finally to the Ulaid at the battle of Airtech. This battle was traditionally fought a generation following the Táin period. Following this, however, they seem to have still ruled 'Connacht' until the coming of the Gaels, who were to finally destroy them. Whether it is factual or not the whole lifestyle portrayed in the Táin cycle is that of a warrior society, therefore based on the influences of the La Tène Culture, and thus Ireland retained in effect until the coming of Christianity a Celtic society uninfluenced by Roman culture, although Gaelic modes of warfare had successfully replaced the archaic chariot warfare of the Gallo-Britons by this time.

As has been said, the earliest known source for the story of Tuathal Techtmar's conquest of Ireland from the Aithech thuatha (Vassal Tribes of non-Gaelic origin, ie Cruthin, Belgae and Domnonians) is the poem by Mael Mura of Othain (AD 885). This set of 83 quatrains was composed for King Flann Sirra who reigned from 879 to 916. The poet intimates that 750 years had elapsed since Tuathal marched on Ancient Tara. Thus Mael Mura dates the invasion about AD 135 and this is probably approximately correct. In Mael Mura's account the standard conventions are employed, however, to make Tuathal an exiled Irishman returning with a foreign army. The account in the *Lebor Gabála* is probably older, and in this we see that

Tuathal was born outside Ireland, and had not seen the country before he invaded it. Both, however, give the definite facts that he came with an army of foreigners to the Eastern coast and conquered the Belgae, Domnonii and Galioin, and an unknown tribe known as the Ligmuini. In doing so he created the Midland Gaelic Colony (Meath), reducing the Lagin to vassalage and imposing on them a heavy tribute. It was not until the eighth century that the Lagin freed themselves from the Gaelic tribute.

The Gaels knew themselves as Feni or land-owning freemen, and I do not think we have to look any further for their place of origin than the north-west of Spain where the Astures Cantabri and Galloeci only surrendered to the Romans under the Caesar Augustus in 27 BC. Thus to this day the Basques, who were recorded in Roman times as Vascones, have retained their ancient non-Indo-European language in this region. The Gaels indeed spoke a very ancient form of Celtic, archaic 'Q-Celtic', and because of this the distortion has been introduced in the Irish context that because they have an archaic tongue they are the ancient people of Ireland. One cannot state too often that this notion is contrary to the oldest traditions of the Gaels themselves. Tovar has identified Q-Celtic inscriptions in Spain and Iberian names abound in Gaelic genealogies and later hagiographical material, for example, Eber Scot compounds Iberus and Scotus, while such names as St Ibar and St Sciath may be derivatives. Seneca of Cordova placed Scotti in Spain in the first century AD and this tribe may well be the Scotraige of the Waterford–Tipperary area whose name the Romans gave to the Irish Gaels in general (cf Graeci for the Hellenes).

Furthermore the name Techtmar itself is a foreign epithet, unique in Irish tradition, and its meaning is lost to us. Tuathal is simply Teutos-valos 'ruler of the people'. As regards the word Gael, this is a derivative of the P-Celtic (Brittonic) speech of the old Welsh Guidel, modern Welsh Gwyddwl for 'Raider' and Goidel did not replace Feni in Irish usage until the latter part of the seventh century at the earliest. Numerous loan-words in old Gaelic show that the British speech (Iarnbelrae or 'Language of the Erainn') contained to be spoken by sections of the population down to the seventh century. It seems not infeasible that the earlier population used a form of the word to describe the new invaders who must have come from Spain, probably as Roman soldiers or auxiliaries. To be described as Gaels must have been tantamount to have been labelled as foreigners, and it is quite reasonable that the colonists should use the name Feni to distinguish themselves from the Vassal Tribes. Only when it again became respectable and the British speech had been erased from Ireland could it have been adopted back from 'Welsh', for by this time the Welsh know of no other Irish but Guidel so that Guidel meant simply Irish, as did Scotti in Latin.

Traditions of the second invasion – that of Munster – have survived in two important early texts. The first occurs among the genealogical material of Laud 610. This is of interest in that it implies quite openly that, when Mug Nuadat (otherwise Eogan) came to Ireland with his foreign warriors, he was doing so for the first time and not as an exile. The later and fuller version of the above tract is found in *Cath Maige Lena*. This follows the standard convention of the pseudo-historians in making Eogan (alias Mug Nuadat) an exile to Spain where he married the daughter of King Eber. After nine years he returns with 2,000 Spanish warriors and the Munster-Erainn (Iverni) submit without a fight. Following this, Eogan instigates a rebellion of Ulaid and Lagin against the contemporary King of the Midland Gaels, Conn of the Hundred battles. Thus, the story tells, Ireland was divided between the Eóganachta and the Connachta. And, forever after, Gaelic literature describes the Northern half of Ireland as Leth Cuinn (Conn's Half) and the Southern Half as Leth Moga (Mug's Half). Such names, however, could not have actually come into being until the Gaelic invasion was well advanced. The Gaelic occupation of the whole of Ireland was to take several centuries.

According to Laud 610, the date reckoned for Tuathal's becoming King of Ireland (actually King of Tara) is AD 153. This approximates to Mael Mura's reckoning of AD 135. According to the pedigrees of the Gaelic Kings we see that Tuathal is ten generations earlier than Loegaire mac Neill, who died in AD 462 or 463. This again corresponds to the above figures. Again Mug Nuadat is represented as a rival of Conn, whose reign began in AD 199, according to Laud 610. Conn is traditionally Tuathal's grandson, so that our dates still appear logical. Finally Mug Nuadat, according to the pedigrees, lived eight generations before Angus mac Nad Froich who died about AD 490, and thus Mug must have flourished about AD 200. All the dates of pre-Christian kings are of course approximate, and the names of many of the kings in the regnal lists and pedigrees seem to belong to mythology. However, because of the obvious importance of the first Gaelic kings in Ireland, it would seem feasible that at least the number of generations since such an event would be recorded accurately in a culture well-known for its adherence to oral tradition. Whatever the date of its inception, the Midland Colony of Meath was to become the centre of Gaelic expansion under Tuathal Techtmar and his descendants. Independently the Eóganacht were to expand in the South. Though it may be propaganda, the story goes that the southern settlement among the Belgae was peaceful, for that people were much reduced by famine and Mug Nuadat helped them to overcome it.

Meanwhile, in Britain, the government seems to have been carried on in peace, and since there were no dangers or troubles to excite even the mere attention of Rome, we may assume that the Roman Province prospered. Two or three inscriptions found in different parts of 'England' refer distinctly to this period, and, as they relate chiefly to dedications and restorations of buildings, they seem to confirm our supposition that the island remained at peace. One of these, relating to the re-building of a temple and raised by the troop of Austurians stationed at Cilumun, shows us that, under the reign of Heliogabalus, Marius Valerianus was Governor of Britannia in AD 221. Another inscription, found in Cumberland, shows that the Governor of the Emperor Gordian in the year 243 was Nonnius Philippus.

Amidst the anarchy and disorder of the reign of Gallienus (AD 260–268), a number of usurpers arose in different parts of the Empire. These were popularly known as The Thirty Tyrants, of whom Lollianus, Victorinus, Postumus, the two Tetrici and Marius are believed to have assumed the sovereignty in Britain. Britain must therefore have become again the theatre of unrest. Yet, though ready enough to rise in support of their own leaders, the Roman troops in Britain seemed to have ignored appeals from outside. When an officer in the Continental Army named Bonosus, who, although born in Spain, was descended from a family in Britain, proclaimed himself emperor in the reign of Aurelian, and appealed for support from the western troops, he found them unresponsive. The frequency of usurpations within the island itself, however, seems to show a desire among the inhabitants to form an independent state. This desire came to fruition in the reign of the joint Emperors Diocletian and Maximian, which commenced in the year AD 284. This reign was rendered remarkable chiefly by the successful usurpation of Carausius, and the first mention of the nomenclature Pict for the Caledonian Kindred, while their old name of Caledonians, and the more recent one of Maeatae, are less used. Associated with increasing predatory raids by the Picts, the eastern and south-eastern coasts of Britain began to be troubled by German seafarers from the mouth of the Elbe. To oppose the latter it was found necessary not only to erect a line of fortresses along the coast, but to establish and maintain a strong fleet centred at Gessoriacum (Boulogne), with the ports on the coast of Kent, Sussex and Hampshire.

Among the officers of this fleet was a Manapian named Carausius, who, by immense naval talent, rose to the position of Admiral of the British Fleet. Carausius used quickly the well-known maxim that the best form of defence is attack and seems to have become more or less a prey on the Germans rather than the reverse. He soon acquired great wealth and thus became a threat to Maximian, who sent orders for him to be assassinated. Carausius appears to have been popular with both army and navy, and was able to proclaim himself the equal of Maximian and Diocletian by declaring an alliance with the Franks and other German tribes. Controlling the channel from Gessoriacum, Carausius held the supreme power in Britain for nearly seven years (AD 287–293). In AD 292, however, Maximian and Diocletian strengthened their government by the appointment of two Caesars, Constantius Chlorus and Galvius. The provinces of the Western Empire fell to the lot of Constantius Chlorus, who marched without delay to attack Carausius in Gessoriacum. Carausius, who was in Gessoriacum when Constantius arrived there, took sail for Britain.

Gessoriacum soon surrendered to the Imperial forces, but it was four years later before Constantius could build a fleet capable of transporting his troops to Britain, and at the same time matching the rebel navy. In the meantime, however, in the year 293, Carausius was murdered by his own naval commander, Allectus, who assumed the rebel imperial authority. At last, however, in AD 296, Constantius had completed his preparations and the invasion of Britain began. The principal force of Constantius, under the able command of the Prefect Asclepiodotus, eluded the fleet of Allectus in thick fog and destroyed both him and his army in the first battle on landing. The Caesar Constantius then took up residence in York, and in a panegyric to him written in AD 297 we first hear the name Pict applied to the Northern people. It may have been during the following period that Irish raiders also began to harass Roman Britannia. Foremost among these were the Lagin, who appear to have colonised Anglesey and the Llynn Peninsula of Caernarvonshire. The place name Llynn (older Lleyn), along with a few others in the area, such as Dinllaen and Mallaen, have been explained as containing either the normative plural or genitive plural forms of Lagin. These people were indeed the first vassals of the Gaels, their first mercenary tribes and the first to be accorded the accolade of Gaelic ancestry by the synthetic historians. It may have been these people who were driven later from North Wales by the Votaddini (Gododdin) in the form of Cunedda and his sons. If Cunedda did drive them back to Ireland they would have to be found 'lebensraum' and they obviously did. The precise time of these events we do not yet know. The eventual losers at all events were to be the Ancient Kindred of the fifth century.

In the year 305, with the resignation of Diocletian and Maximian, Constantius and Galvius assumed command of the Roman Empire. Now Constantius was the father of Constantine the Great, and at the time of his father's accession to the Empire, Constantine was serving under Gallerius at Nicomedia. Constantine escaped quickly from Gallerius, and having joined his father at Gessoriacum, they both crossed to Britain and assumed the government. Following an expedition against "the Caledonians and other Picts", Constantius became ill and died at York on 25 July 305. Constantine was immediately proclaimed emperor by the army, and Galerius reluctantly acknowledged him as the sovereign of the provinces beyond the Alps. Constantine married Fausta the daughter of Maximian in the following year and consolidated his dominions. His future history of becoming sole master of the Roman Empire, of instituting Christianity as the State religion and of re-naming Byzantium as Constantinople belong to World History. What was important to Britain, however, was the appearance of a fully organised British Church at the Synod of Arles in AD 314 and, whatever the course of persecution, by the close of the fourth century Christianity must have prevailed universally among the Brittonic peoples. In 337, however, when preparing to march against the Persians, Constantine fell ill at Nicomedia, and died there in his sixty-fourth year. He was baptised on his death bed by Eusebius, and to his three sons fell the inheritance of the Roman Empire.

Among the Roman historians in the fourth century Ammianus Marcellinus stands pre-eminent, and his works are highlighted by the poems of his friend Claudian. The Gaels seem to have begun their conflict in earnest with the Romans as early as 343. So we now see a new name for Irish raiders becoming prominent in the Latin Scotti, and Ireland becomes known as Scotia. In AD 364 the Picts, Scotti and Attacotti descended in concert but by different ways (per diversa vagantes) on Roman territory. The Picts in this age were divided into two great tribes, the Dicalidones (Caledonians) and Verturiones. The Attacotti were P-Celtic tribes, and may well have included, or have wholly been, the Aithech Tuath or Vassal Tribes of Cruthin. They settled in south-western Scotland, becoming known as Picts. On the eastern coast the Saxons were also becoming every day more formidable. Eventually in 369 the Emperor Valentian entrusted the task of re-organising the country's defences to the ablest of his imperial generals, the celebrated Theodosius. It is quite evident from the old historian's account that Theodosius had to contend with an insurrection of the subject Britons as well as the invasion. Thus he issued a proclamation offering a pardon to "all who would desert from their ranks and on this promise a great number returned to their duty". Ammanius incidentally blames Valentian himself for a habitual inattention to the complaints of his subjects in the distant provinces, and informs us that it was this which had caused the trouble in Britain. He also tells us that Theodosius was forced to abolish the Roman Secret Service (Arcani) in Britain because they had collaborated with the enemy and had provided information which had enabled the enemy to time their invasions. After clearing the invaders from the southern territory, Theodosius recovered the territory between the walls of Hadrian and Antoninus, and gave them to the new province he made of it the name of Valentia. Among the auxiliary troops sent to Britain was a body of Germans (numerous Alemannorum) with a chief (rex) named Fraomarius with the rank of Tribune. Settlements of Germans such as these were to be the vanguard of later colonisation by Angles, Saxons and Jutes, although the Belgae themselves may well have been Germanic people under Celtic-speaking over-lords.

In 383, during the reign of Gratian in the West, a native of Spain named Magnus Maximus was "made emperor in Britain through the treachery of the soldiers" according to a fifth century Gaulish chronicle. Maximus

(Macsen), with the help of the British troops, overcame Gaul and Spain before being killed in 388. At about this time the Deisi, who were in origin Fir Bolg, were forced to migrate en masse from south-east Ireland to Pembroke in Wales, and the Ui Liathain from Cork settled west of them in Gower and west Glamorgan. Thus were the Belgae forced back again to Britain. How many of them spoke Gaelic and how many the old Brittonic Language of the Erainn we shall never know. The tombstone of their first king, Eochaid Over-Sea, survives with his name in British and Irish Ogham. Coupled with later migrations to Cornwall, it is by no means improbable that the numbers of Irish, Gael and non-Gael, living in Western Britain exceeded the various Germans on the East until the sixth century.

However, to return to our story, the withdrawal of the troops guarding the northern frontiers by Magnus Maximus was the signal for a descent of the Picts on the Northern Wall, and, with its destruction, it was never rebuilt. Due to the powerful General Stilicho, a Vandal, during the period AD 395–400 contemporary panegyrists maintain that Britain had no fear of Pict, Saxon or Scot (Irishman). In 401, however, Stilicho was forced to withdraw his troops to fight the Goths who were now threatening the Empire. His place was taken by various usurpers, the last of whom, Constantine, also crossed to Gaul to secure the Rhine, and was killed in 411 at Arles at the bidding of the Emperor Honorius. The Britons appealed to Honorius for help, but he replied in 409 that they would have to look after themselves.

The earliest known Irish Gaelic is inscribed on Ogham stones, which have been found in greatest quantities on the lands of the Corcu Duibne of the Kerry peninsulae and of the Deisi in Waterford, but also throughout Ireland. The Ogham alphabet is based upon the Latin one, and is schematised into a system of strokes and dots. Since the Latin alphabet fits poorly to Gaelic, the Ogham must have originated in the Latin cultural province, and, indeed, similar inscriptions are found in western Britain with the Gaelic messages sometimes accompanied by translations in Brittonic and Vulgar Latin. The conclusion is, therefore, that Ogham was introduced into Ireland via the Vassal Tribes of Deisi who settled in western Britain, but who left remnants of their tribes in Munster. They also indicate, for the first time, the predominance of the Gaelic speech among those peoples during the periods indicated. From this point readers must beware of identifying the Gaels proper (Feni) with their Gaelic-speaking vassals, genealogically produced 'kinsmen' and still intransigent foes. The existing native documentary evidence on Ireland is Gaelic inspired. Thus if this evidence intimates in the slightest that the dominant Feni were relatively recent settlements, we must respect it the more. Furthermore, conservative Celtic culture maintained an oral tradition and abhorred the written word. The tolerance exhibited by the Waterford Scotraige to the Ogham innovation obviously extended only to the Gaelic language itself.

Mercifully the veil of legend, mythology and propaganda has been partially lifted from the history of Ireland, and we can now give dates of which we are fairly certain. Any dates prior to AD 400 are at best approximations and at worst pure fabrications. We do know that Eochaid Mugmedon ruled the Midland Gaels towards the end of the fourth century. Of his reign we know nothing except that he raided Britain, for there is good evidence that his wife Cairenn (Carina) was a Brittonic captive, so that his famous son Niall of the Nine Hostages was half-British in blood. Niall reigned Tara during the first quarter of the fifth century until about AD 427. He became famous for his raids on Roman Britannia, and probably met his death on one of these. For the following six centuries the self-styled 'Kings of Ireland' were descended from Niall and we know them as the 'Uí Néill'. By the end of Niall's reign the political map of Ireland was drastically altered, although for how much of this he was personally responsible we shall probably never know. Three 'brothers' from among the Connachta – Brian, Fiacha and Aillil – had invaded the ancient province of Ol Nechnacht and utterly destroyed the Domnainn (Domnonians). In the whole of central and southern Ulster were a number of vassal states known to us now by the collective name of the Airgialla (Oriel). Among these 'hostage-givers' were the Airthir, the Uí Chrimthainn, Uí Meith, Uí Thuirtri, Mugdornai and the Uí Mac Uais. In north-west Ulster Niall's son Enda established his own Gaelic kingdom. The territory of the Venniconian Cruthin, Clan Connall, now Donegal, became known as Tir-Connall (the Land of Connall), and from Connall was descended the O'Donnells. Donegal was thoroughly gaelicised and the autonomous Cruthin dynasties driven east. The territory of another King Eogan (Owen) was Inishowen (the island of Owen). The Clan Owen later expanded into Tir Owen, which is now called Tyrone. From Owen descended the northern O'Neills, the McLoughlins, O'Kanes,

O'Hagans, O'Mullans, Devlins and other Gaelic-speaking peoples. Loegaire and Niall's remaining sons stayed in control of the Midlands, and it was this King Loegaire whom Patrick is said to have met.

The original dynasties of Ulster were mostly confined now to the area comprised mostly of the present counties of Antrim and Down. This territory alone maintained the right to be known as Ulster (Gaelic Ulaidh = Latin Ulidia). So long as the dynasty of the Ulaid survived, even in an attenuated form, the Gaelic Uí Néill could not style themselves Kings of Ulster. The independent territories became known by the names of the gaelicised ruling families (Dál = a portion). Of the Ulaid there remained only the Dál Fiatach of County Down, while their Erainnian kinsmen the Dál Riata were confined to the north-eastern portion of Antrim. Dál Riata (Dalriada, Dalreuda) comprised that area of Antrim between the Giant's Causeway and Glenarm Bay, while the Ulaid retained the sovereignty of the maritime area of Down. It is also beyond doubt that many of the inhabitants of the territories of Dál Riata and Dál Fiatach were actually Cruthin. The name Riata may even derive from the Robogdian Cruthin. The Manapii (Fermanagh) and their kinsmen the Brigantes (Uí Bairrche) now dwelled mostly in Ulster, mainly in the Mourne Country of South Down where they had been driven by Laginian and Gaelic pressure, although a remnant of the Fermanagh remained on the shores of Lough Erne and in Taughmonagh, now Belfast. Here then was to be ended that fierce independence whose flame burned so brightly against the Romans.

It was, however, the Cruthin who formed the bulk of the population of Old Ulidia. The autonomous Cruthinic territory comprised most of the area of Antrim and Down, but extended also from Loch Foyle to Dundalk Bay. The name of the main dynasty was Dál n Araidi, and the state they founded became Dalaradia in English. This must not be confused with Belgic Dalriada in the north-east. There is evidence, however, of the existence of from seven to nine minor kingdoms of the Cruthin in the whole area until the sixth century, the dominant one in the seventh being the Uí Chóelbad. North-west of the Lower Bann dwelled the Cruthin of Arda Eolarig and the Li. The northern Dál n Araidi extended from Lough Neagh northwards to the sea between the mouths of the rivers Bush and Bann, and included Coleraine, and its environs, which are now County Londonderry. They also inhabited the area east of the Bann to the sea at Larne, which bore the name Latharna. In Down the Southern Cruthin (Uí Echach Cobha) inhabited the present baronies of Upper and Lower Iveagh and Kinelarty. The boundary between Airgialla (Oriel) and the remnant of Ulster (Ulidia) was made permanent by a remarkable earthen wall running along the vale of the Newry River. Part of this earthwork, known erroneously as the 'Dane's Cast', can be seen to this day. It extends from Lisnagade one mile north-east of Scarva in Down, to near Meigh, not far from Killeavy, and Slieve Gullion in Armagh. In construction it consists of a wide fosse or trench with a rampart on either side. The numerous raths and duns on the eastern side show that the area was densely populated by a strong military force. The chief fortifications were at Lisnagade, Fathom, Crown Mound, Tierney and Listullyard. Next to Lisnagade, Fathom must have been the most important place since it commands Moiry Pass. This defence system was to remain politically effective for 200 years.

The invasion of the Midland Gaels into Ulster, and the destruction of the sovereignty of the Ulaid, was to change the course of World History. The population movements which ensued resulted in settlements of Dalriadan Scots along the western seaboard of Britain, mainly Argyll and its island. Bede, writing in the eighth century (*A History of the English Church and People*) states that this land was obtained from the Picts by a combination of force and treaty. There does not seem, however, to have been a full-scale invasion and the bulk of the ordinary people of modern Argyll remained as Epidian Cruthin. These Scots gave their name to Scotland and, when their royal dynasty, in the person of Fergus mac Erc, forsook the Irish Capital of Dunseverick about AD 500 and took up residence in Scottish Dalriada, we may assume that by this time the colony had ousted the mother-country in importance. The second point is that the fifth and sixth centuries are known to have been a period of unusually rapid development in the Gaelic language, as shown by the contrast between the general language of Ogham inscriptions and the earliest Old Gaelic known from manuscripts. There is little doubt that this was due to the widespread adoption of the Gaelic speech by the original inhabitants and the passage of Brittonic loan words into Gaelic. This process was accelerated by the awarding of Gaelic ancestry to the Dál Riata, who forever afterwards knew themselves only as Gaels. At this point therefore only the Cruthin preserved their non-Gaelic origins, although among them too Gaelic became the common tongue.

There is nothing more certain, however, in the whole early history of Ireland, than that the Dál Riata were Erainn (Iverni, Fir Bolg), and therefore non-Gaelic in origin.

In AD 398 St Ninian had planted the first Christian Church in what is now Scotland at Candida Casa (now Whithorn) in Galloway. Although little is known about this great Saint of the Novantes, or the earliest history of his foundation, it is clear that in the fifth and sixth centuries Candida Casa was an important centre of evangelism to both Britain and Northern Ireland. Of the history of Christianity in Ireland there are many texts which are very learned and above any criticism which I might dare to make. There are a few points however which are seldom emphasised. Of that Patrick who wrote the *Confession* and *Letter to Coroticus* we have evidence of a great and holy man who loved the Scriptures. The holy Patrick was brought in slavery to Ireland from Romanised Britain and sold to a chieftain called Michu, who used him to tend his livestock around Mount Slemish in County Antrim. Milchu was of the Cruthin and thus Patrick came not among the Gaels proper (Feni) but among the Cruthin. It is said that after six years of slavery he escaped, but returned about AD 432 to preach the gospel. They also say he stopped first at Wicklow, but not getting a good reception came north and landed in County Down in the territory of Dichu (of the Ulaid) who became his first convert. Dichu's barn (sabhall or Saul) near Downpatrick was the first of his churches. Patrick makes a clear distinction between the Scotti (Gaels) and the original peoples, the Hibernians (Cruthin and Ulaid). We can easily discern the old name of Ierne in the latter name. When Armagh (Ard Macha) was founded in AD 444 as the chief church in Ireland, Emain Macha (now Navan Fort) may still have been the political centre of the North.

Among Patrick's first converts were Bronach, daughter of Milchu and her son Mochaoi (Mahee). St Mochaoi was to found the great monastery of Nendrum on Mahee Island in Loch Cuan (Strangford Lough), and is associated with Patrick in the legends which grew around his name. These firmly place Down as a cradle of Christianity in Ireland. At Nendrum were first educated Colman, who was of the Cruthin, and Finnian (British Uinniau), who was of the Dál Fiatach (Ulaid). Colman founded in the early sixth century the famous See of Dromore in Iveagh (Cruthin) while Finnian, following a visit to Candida Casa, founded the great school of

Movilla (Newtownards) in Down. Finnian is also notable for bringing the first copy of the Scriptures to Ireland. Even without knowing the personalities involved it is scarcely surprising that the territory nearest to Galloway should be the first to feel the evangelising influences of Candida Casa. Yet it was in Bangor in North Down that the highest ideals of the Cruthin were to be realised. Founded in AD 555 on Ulidian territory by Comgall, perhaps the most famous of all the Cruthin, the monastery of Bangor was to become the centre of literature, both sacred and secular, in the sixth and seventh centuries. Here was to be compiled in all probability the original *Chronicles of Ireland*, and the beautiful poetry *The Voyage of Bran*. In the region also those old traditions of the Ulaid were preserved which were moulded into the Gaelic masterpiece *Táin Bó Cúailgne*. The ancient Ulster chronicle has been attributed to Sinlan Moccu Min, who as Sinlanus is described in the list of abbots in the Bangor Antiphonary as the "famed teacher of the world" (famosus mundi magister). This document may be seen in the Ambrosian Library of Milan today.

Both Movilla and Bangor were great centres of scholarship, and in the sixth century many of the great scholars and saints of Ireland were educated in one or other of them. Columba, who was said, probably falsely, to have been of the House of the Uí Néill, studied under St Finnian at Movilla, and Comgall of Bangor helped them in his work among the Picts of Alba (Modern Scotland). Columba founded in AD 563 the religious centre of Iona, which was to be cultural apotheosis of Scotland and where some scholars think the magnificent *Book of Kells* was executed. This may be seen in the Trinity College, Dublin. The followers of Columba were composed of all the peoples of Ireland, united in religion. Yet we can see by Adomnán's *Life of Columba* that the Cruthin were still considered non-Gaelic at this time. This was doubtless because of the powerful kinship of the Pictish Kingdom of North Britain. From the Bangor Monastery were also to come Columbanus, who founded Luxeuil in France and Bobbio in Italy, and St Gall, after whom a Monastery and Canton of that name was founded in Switzerland. These were to be the chief centres of scholarship and religion which brought Europe at last out of the 'Dark Ages'.

Subject to continuing aggression by the Uí Néill and internal dissension, the Cruthin and Ulaid were to further decline in Ireland, and the focus of their history was to be changed to North Britain. An event of the greatest significance is recorded in the *Annals of Ulster*, dated AD 562. We see that in AD 563 the Cruthin were defeated at the Battle of Moin-daire-Lothair by the "Uí Néill of the North". The opposing armies were led, on the one side by "seven kings of the Cruthin including Hugh (Brecc)", and on the other side by one Baetan with two kings of the Cruthin in alliance with the "Northern Uí Néill". The latter, Clan Connall, who were in reality gaelicised Cruthin, and Clan Owen, were rewarded with the territory of Lei (Ballymoney) and Arda Eolairg. The influence of Columba in the following events cannot be over-estimated. As presumably an important member of the Uí Néill and the greatest ecclesiastic in Ireland his position was unique. Though he was not above using their temporal power for his own ends, as shown by the Battle of Cuildrevne in AD 561, Columba exercised a restraining influence on the Uí Néill. To Columba (his kinsman through the female line) we can attribute much of the greatness of Aedan, great-grandson of Fergus Mor and King of Dalriada from AD 574 to about 608. Aedan is known to have fought battles in Ireland, in the Isle of Man, in the Orkneys, in the Pictish province of Circinn and against the Maeatae of central Scotland. His son Arthur may well have been that hero who has survived in legend as King Arthur of Camelot. Another interesting parallel is that Cuchulain became Sir Gawain and the Knights of the Round Table are modelled on the Red Branch Champions of Ulster.

According to Adomnán (d 704), Columba crowned Aedan King of Dalriada on Iona. Since Columba had won the friendship of Bridei (Brude), King of the Picts (d 584), and converted him to Christianity, Iona (according to Bede) "held for a long time pre-eminence over the monasteries of all the Picts, and was their superior in ruling their communities". Thus Iona became the centre of the Scottish-Irish Cultural Province. Columba's friendship with Aedan was of paramount importance for both Church and State in Dalriada. He advised Aedan at the Convention of Druim Cett in AD 575, when Aedan refused to pay tribute to Hugh, son of Ainmire, King of the Uí Néill. In his relations with the Cruthin of Dál n Araidi, with whom he was not apparently related, Columba shows on the other hand the prejudices of a scion of the Gaelic Uí Néill. About AD 579 there appears to have been a dispute between Columba and Comgall about a church near Coleraine. This resulted in a battle at Coleraine between the Cruthin and the Uí Néill, an event difficult to understand by anyone unaware of the ethnic differences in the Irish population, complicated by dynastic ambitions from which the Ecclesiastics were far from immune.

In AD 597 the great Columba died on Iona, and in 603 Comgall of the Cruthin died in Bangor. Thus passed away two of the finest spirits of an age. History had been less kind to Comgall, for his name was to decline for a season. Lacking Columba's counsel, Aedan was defeated by the Northumbrian Angles at an unidentified battle of Degsastan in 603. The result of this decisive battle was to clear a way for the Angles both to Lothian in the North and to Galloway and Dumfries in the West. South-western Scotland was still occupied by the Cumbrian Britons, who knew themselves distinctively as Brython and included remnants of the Brigantes, Selgovae and Novantes. The 'Welsh Triads' (eighth century) name the two other Brittonic peoples, the dominant Cymry and the Lloegrwys. The Cymry (Cimbri) stood for the Belgae and survived as the Welsh. The Lloegrwys were "deprived of their government" by the Coranied (Cruthin) and Saxons. "All the Lloegrwys became Saxons, except those who are found in Cornwall [Domnonii] and in the commot of Caenovan in Deira and Bernicia". There was thus no memory of the Lloegrian Domnonii of Ayrshire.

By the end of the Roman period, the beginning of the fifth century, the Brittonic peoples had evolved into primitive states. The most clearly to emerge are Strathclyde (Arecluta) Rheged (Reget) and Elmet. At the eastern end of the Forth-Clyde isthmus lay Guotodin (Gododdin), the country of the Votaddini, which covered Lothian and most of the Eastern Lowlands. The region of Manau of the Gododdin lay in the environs of Stirling and both Stirling and Edinburgh were Gododdin strongholds. About the year 600 the Gododdin, aided by other champions among the 'Gwyr y Gogledd' or 'Men of the North' sent an expedition under Mynyddog against the 'Men of Lloegr', ie the English occupied provinces of Dewr (Deira = Yorkshire) and Brynaich (Bernicia = Northumberland and Durham). The defeat and annihilation of the Brittonic allies at Catraeth (perhaps Catterick in Yorkshire) is recorded in the great Poem of Aneirin, *The Gododdin*. The further defeat of Aedan's Scots by Aethelfrith of Bernicia at Degsastan, therefore, was a significant event for the Britons also, since it spelled the collapse of the kingdom of Gododdin and allowed the English plantation of Lothian which was to follow. In AD 605 Aethelfrith made himself King of Deira also and fused the two kingdoms into the State of Northumbria, which he ruled until he died in 617.

In AD 627 Congal Claen (One-Eye), Prince of the Uí Chóelbad Cruthin, became over-king of Old Ulidia. He had ruled in Tara until his blinding by bees put him from his kingship. The following year he slew the Uí Néill high-king, Suibne Menn of the Clan Owen. In 629 Congal's Cruthin slew the King of Dalriada and his Bernician guests. This seems to have resulted in the Battle of Dun Ceithirnn in Londonderry later that year, when the Uí Néill under their new high-king Domnall, son of Hugh, defeated Congal and crushed the Cruthin. Congal fled to Scotland where he succeeded in reversing the Dalriadan alliance with the Northern Uí Néill. In 637 he returned with a large army under Domnall Brecc, Aedan's grandson. In that year, therefore, was fought the famous battle of Mag Rath (Moira) in County Down against Domnall, son of Hugh, by the allies of Old Ulidia. Congal was killed and Domnall Brecc lost his Ulster territories. Thus did the Uí Néill consolidate their power in Ulster. About 642 Domnall Brecc was killed by the Britons of Cumbria at the Battle of Strathcarron "and the head of Domnall Brecc, ravens gnawed it". So wrote the Britons, but let his epitaph speak also for the fall of the Great Wall of Ulidia. The *Annals of the Four Masters* record that in AD 665, the Battle of Farset took place between the County Down Ulaid and the Cruthin, where Cathasach, son of Laircine, was slain. This was an attempt by the Ulaid to encroach on the Cruthin territory of Trian Congail, the 'third of Congal', which encompassed territory on both sides of the Lagan, corresponding more or less to Upper and Lower Clandeboye, including modern Belfast. Cathasach was Congal's grandson. The battle was the first mention of Belfast in Irish history. Unmarked is the grave of Congal Claen but his memory will live forever, for he was the last autonomous Cruthinic king to provide an effective opposition to the Gaels in Ulster.

CHAPTER 4

THE GALLS

THE FURTHER HISTORY OF the former peoples may be read in many texts. By the AD 670s the Picts, Scots and Cumbrian Britons had all come under the power of the Northumbrian Angles. This overlordship was brought to an end by Bridei, King of the Picts, when he defeated the Angles (English) at the Battle of Nechtansmere (Dunnichen) in AD 685. Bridei's victory, as Bede, who was a contemporary and interested witness, has made clear, was a turning point in the early history of North Britain. It destroyed the power of the Angles in the Lowlands of Scotland and enabled the Picts to regain much of their ancient territory. Already in the lifetime of Adomnán (d 704), the Ulster-Scottish kingdom of Argyll (Dalriada) had "come under the power of its enemies." Pictish Expansion culminated in 741 with "the smiting of Dalriada by Angus, son of Fergus", King of all the Picts.

The traditional understanding of the history of the ancient Venniconian Kingdoms of Donegal maintained that at some time in the late fifth century the sons of Niall of the Nine hostages, Caipre, Conaill, Enda and Eogan had launched an invasion into that territory from Tara, having defeated and conquered the indigenous people, or more probably the rulers of those people. The four brothers were said to have divided out the territory of Donegal between them and each then established a kingdom which subsequently bore his name. In one form or another these kingdoms were believed to have lasted for all of the early medieval period.

Collectively these kingdoms were never ever linked but we know them now as the 'Northern Uí Néill', who went on to conquer the rest of western and central Ulster. Two of the kingdoms, Clan Connal (Cenél Conaill) and Clan Owen (Cenél nÉogan), were said to be the most dominant, so that for about three centuries after their establishment, the kingship of the whole territory was shared between them. In addition, when each of their kings was ascendant, they respectively claimed ownership of the prestigious kingship of Tara, which has been claimed to have had some sort of overriding national influence. The ancient extent of Tírowen's influence included the whole of the present counties of Tyrone and Londonderry, and the four baronies of West Inishowen, East Inishowen, Raphoe North and Raphoe South in County Donegal.

As we now know, however, this whole story is a later propagandistic fiction, rather than a summary of what actually happened. Almost certainly it was given its classical form by and on behalf of the Clan Owen during the reign in the mid-eighth century of their powerful and ambitious king, Aed (Hugh) Allan, who died in the year 743. Whatever his actual victories and political successes, they were emphasised by a set of deliberately created fictional historical texts which reported to give him and his ancestors a more glorious past than they had actually enjoyed. The same texts projected his dynasty back to the dawn of history and created a new political relationship with the neighbouring kingdoms. Whatever the initial reaction to them, these political fictions were plausible enough to endure and have been ultimately accepted as history by most historians, including modern Gaelic propagandists ('serious scholars'), over the past 1300 years. Aed's pseudo-historians were probably led by the Armagh Bishop Congus, who exploited the opportunity provided by the alliance with the King to advance the case for the supremacy of his own church of Armagh throughout Ireland. Congus himself was from Cul Athguirt in the Parish of Islandmagee, County Antrim. He was descended from Dá Slúaig, the son of Ainmire, so he was a member of the Húi Nadsluaga clan, who were one of the primthúatha of the Cruthin Dál mBuinne (Dalmunia or Dalboyn), east of Lough Neagh. He was a scribe and advisor to Aed before being elevated to the See of Armagh, and he instigated the Battle of Fochairt for his own personal advancement. He died in 750.

With the weakening of English power in Galloway, the Old Ulidians migrated there in increasing numbers from the dominance of the Uí Néill. Migration from Antrim and Down may have begun in the sixth and early seventh centuries, as is evidenced by isolated archaeological finds from Galloway indicating changes in ritual practices (log coffin burials), the spread of a type of early ecclesiastical site (the enclosed, developed cemetery, which is regarded as Irish-inspired), and other minor pointers in the same direction. It is also highly likely that the Cruthin were those invading tribes known as Goidel ffichti (ie Pictish Gaels or Irish Picts) by the North Britons. It is of extreme significance, however, that from AD 774 onwards the name Cruthin ceases to be written for a section of the Irish population in the *Annals of Ulster*, and only the dynastic name of Dál n Araidi is applied to the area of East Antrim and Down we know to have been inhabited by them. And, whatever may have been the defeats of their earlier attempts, the Cruthin, at the end of the eighth century, made a successful settlement within the Rhinns of Galloway. Strengthened by Kindred Scots from Kintyre (Epidian Cruthin), they occupied over the next two centuries the whole area from the Solway to the Clyde, superimposing Gaelic place names on the old Brittonic ones. Notwithstanding the naval enterprises of the Norse, the incursions of the Northumbrian Danes, and not a few internal distractions among conflicting tribes, the settlers retained in their new possessions the various rights of a distinct people and preserved the agreeable independence of their own laws. Thus did the Ulster Cruthin become known to history as the 'Picts called Galwegians'. The name Cruthin, Cruithne or Cruithnigh survived in the Lowland Scots language as Creenie or Kreenie, which means a servant or working man of Galloway.

The end of the eighth century was a hard time for the Cruthin in Ulster. The *Annals of Ulster* record it thus:

"AD 775 [corrected 776] a battle among the Dál n Araidi themselves at Slemish mountain [Lower Antrim] in which Nia, son of Cualta, was slain. A battle of Drung, again in the same year, among the Dál n Araidi, in which fell Kenneth Cairgge, son of Cathasach, and Dungal, grandson of Fergus Forcraidh. Tomaltach, son of Indrechtach and Echaidh, son of Fiachna, were victors. The battle of Ath-duma between the Airthera and the Ui Echach-Cobha, in which fell Gormgall, son of Conall Crui, King of the Cobha [Cruthin]. AD 776 [corrected 777] The 'bloody flux' [ie Typhoid]. Many diseases besides; a mortality almost. The great mortality of cows."

Expansion of the 'Gaelic' Clan Owen into Airgiallan territory led to an infiltration of the Airgiallan Uí Thuirtri into Dál n Araidi. The depopulation of Cruthinic territory also allowed an expansion of the Dál Fiatach northwards across to the shores of Lough Neagh, thus separating the Cruthin of Dál n Araidi from those of Uí Echach Cobha (Iveagh). Yet for all that in AD 784 the *Annals of Ulster* record the death of Coisennech "nepos Predeni", King of the Iveagh Cruthin. The existence of this pre-Gaelic family name, Predeni (Pretani), so late in Irish history is astonishing, and shows how tenacious the Cruthin were to the memories of their former greatness.

And now there was "devastation of all the islands of Britain by Gentiles". On the east coast of Britain the Danes (dubh gall, 'dark strangers') attacked the Anglian monastery of Lindisfarne in AD 793. On the west coast the Norse (finn gall, 'fair strangers') sacked the Scots monastery of Iona in 795. In 811 the Ulaid had their first taste of Norse Vikings and defeated them. In 823 the Norse returned to destroy and pillage Bangor Monastery, and in 825 they raided Downpatrick and Movilla, but fortunately were eventually badly beaten by the Ulaid in Leth Cathail (Lecale). Then a final attempt by the Ulaid to stop the Clan Owen families (eg the Devlins) from stealing the lands of the Airgialla resulted in the battle of Leth Cam in 827. The victor was Niall mac Hugh, King of the Clan Owen, but self-styled King of Old Ulidia, and the many kings of the Airgialla who were killed. Leth Cam settled the fate of the Airgialla, who became vassals of Ailech under the puppet kings of Airthir.

The story of the Scandinavian (Lochlan) settlements which now occurred in Ireland and Scotland is too often told from a one-sided viewpoint. Early raiding gave way to settlements and such trade and commerce notable in the Danish settlements of Dublin, Wexford, Waterford, Limerick and Cork, and fine literature as exemplified by the *Sagas of the Norse Kings*. Interaction between 'stranger' Gall and 'native' Gael produced in many areas a mixed people known as Vikingr Scotr to the former and Gall-ghaedil to the latter. The interaction is evident in such Celtic names as Njal (Niall = Neill) among the Icelanders. In AD 837 a large Scandinavian fleet arrived on the Boyne and the Liffey, and the leadership of the raiding parties was assumed by the great Viking Thorgestr (Gaelic Turgeis = Latin Turgesius). In 839 Thorgestr brought a fleet to Lough Neagh (Loch n Echach Cobha) and pillaged the north-east. Finally in 841 the ecclesiastical capital of Armagh was pillaged and the plunder helped to establish Danish Dublin. For our purposes the main Norse settlements were in the Shetlands, Orkneys and North Scotland, threatening Pictavia; in the Western Highlands and

Islands, threatening Dalriada of the Scots and Iona; along the coasts of the Solway Firth threatening Galloway; and on the shores of Lough Cuan, now Strangford (Strangfjord) and Carlingford (Carlingfjord) Loughs threatening the Ulidians.

In the AD 840s the Galwegians (Ulster Cruthin) assisted Kenneth Mac Alpin, King of Scots in his battles against the Picts (Caledonian Cruthin) and thus in 844 enabled him to become King of the United Picts and Scots. Kenneth was also assisted by many Lochlans and others from among the Gall-ghaedhil. Gofraid, a Prince of the Airgialla who had settled in Argyle, also came to his aid. Gofraid's people, though at first submerged by Norse sovereignty, were to emerge later as the 'Lords of the Isles'. Kenneth's success, however, was not the annihilation of the Picts which has often been portrayed. Two of the King Lists of Dalriada include among the immediate predecessors of Kenneth the names of several kings of Fortrinn, among them Eoganan Maguinness who is likewise styled 'King of the Dál Riata'. Fortrinn was the land of the Verturiones, whom we have met as a section of the Picts. Thus Kenneth's ascension to the Pictish throne in 844 may have been a rightful one. Another factor is that the Dalriadan 'Scots' must have had many of Ulster Cruthinic stock (Robogdii) among their ranks as well as Erainn. Thus the Picts and Scots differed essentially only in language, and but little in culture at this time. We may be sure that the dynastic and ecclesiastic literati of the Scots (Gaels) soon destroyed what they could of Pictish literature.

During this period, and especially during the latter part of Kenneth's reign (AD 844–860), there was a growth in power of the Gall-gaedhil in Galloway which had begun by Norse incursion along the coasts of the Solway Firth. On the whole Norse suzerainty was benevolent and did not preclude the existence of local chieftains, who ruled over their own people and administered the traditional law. Relations with Kenneth were friendly and this alliance was cemented by the marriage of his daughter to a Norse-Galloway chieftain, Olaf the White. From Gall-gaedhil developed the name of the province, Galwethia, which is derived from the Brittonic form, Galwyddel. However danger threatened from another quarter. In the east the Danes had conquered Anglian Northumbria and in 875, under Halfdan, invaded Brittonic Strathclyde and Cumberland (Cumbria). The devastation they wrought had not been equalled. Carlisle was so utterly destroyed that it remained uninhabited for two centuries. Although the Galwegians were defeated by the Danes at a battle between Castle Douglas and Cross Michael, Danish supremacy was to be only temporary and the Norse were to remain the principal overlords of the Galloway Cruthin. These events are evidenced by archaeology. Thus the 'disc-faced' crosses of Galloway belonging to the early tenth century are moulded by Irish and Viking styles, while in the Lake District, south of the Solway, during the same period there are pure Viking remains, and the dominant Scandinavian influence of the Danes.

Meanwhile the Old Ulidians continued to be threatened by the Uí Néill on the West and by the Norse on the coasts. In AD 912 the Dál Fiatach organised a fleet to combat the Norse, but were defeated by them in a naval action off the English coast, with the loss of their commander, a Prince of Lecale. The following year the Uí Néill invaded Dál n Araidi. Hugh, King of Ulidia, went to the help of his Cruthinic subjects and was defeated after bitter fighting. A peace treaty between Hugh and Niall Glundubh of the Clan Owen, from whom the dynasty of the O'Neills take their name, was made the same year and was ratified at their sacred site at Tullyhog in Tyrone. The result was that, when Niall Glundubh waged war on the Norse, the Ulaid were with him, and Hugh fell with him at the battle of Dublin in 919. By 933 Matudan mac Hugh of the Ulaid raided Monaghan with Norse allies and was routed by the King of Ailech (Matudan is commemorated in Ben Madigan, now Cave Hill outside Belfast). In 942 the Norse raided Downpatrick, but were defeated following a pursuit by the Ulaid. The following year the Ulaid of Lecale exterminated the Norse of Strangford Lough. In 949 Matudan made the fatal mistake of plundering the Cruthin of Conailli Muirthemne, who were the last remnant of that people in Louth and who claimed descent from the great Ulster hero Conall Caernach. Muirthemne was of course Cuchulainn's territory traditionally. The effort was avenged by the Iveagh Cruthin when they slew Matudan the following year. But the increasing weakness of Dál n Araidi is attested by the fact that after 972 they never again provided an over-king of Old Ulidia.

Then again the Uí Néill invaded Antrim. In 1004 a great battle was fought at Craeb Tulcha (Crew Hill, Glenavy). Eochaid Mac Ardgail King of Ulaid, Donnchad King of Dál n Araidi and many of the princes of Old Ulidia were slain. Complete annihilation was averted only by the death in battle of the victor Hugh O'Neill. So many of the Dál Fiatach fell that for three generations there was no acceptable successor to their kingship. The Cruthin in Ulster by this time were so powerless that they themselves could not supply a leader. Now from the South came a call for support against the Lochlans by Brian Boru, greatest of the 'high-kings' of 'Ireland'. But Brian was of the Dál Cais family, kings of Munster and Thomond, and of probable Erainnian origin. His call thus went unanswered in the North because of Ulidian indifference and outright O'Neill animosity. Brian was joined however by two of the South Connacht kingdoms, by the Mor-maer (Earl) of Marr in Scotland and by Melaghlin of the Meath Uí Néill. On the opposing side were the North Lagin and the Danes of Dublin, reinforced by Norse contingents from Man and the Orkneys. Before battle was joined Melaghlin withdrew the Meath army. The battle of Clontarf which ensued on Good Friday 1014, without the help of the treacherous Melaghlin, was the greatest in early Irish history, and is no less famous among the Lochlans as recorded in the *Saga of the Burning of Njal*. It ended in complete victory for the magnificent high-king's army, but personally his complete defeat as well, for Brian himself, his son Murchad and his grandson Turloch were also slain. Rather artificially the battle itself marks the end of the Scandinavian influence in Ireland.

The decline of the Norse influence in Ireland is paralleled by their decline in Galloway. It was not until the thirteenth century that the Hebrides and Isle of Man were abandoned to the crown of Scotland. The Northern Isles of Shetland and Orkney were officially Norwegian until the fifteenth century and until 250 years ago a Scandinavian language 'Norn' was spoken in the Northern Isles, whose influence is present to this day. But in 1043 the death of Suibne son of Kenneth, King of the Galwegians, is recorded showing the growth of the power again of the Pictish Lords of Galloway. The suzerainty was still held, however, by the great Norse jarl Thorfinn the Skullsplitter, whose influence remained strong over a large part of Scotland and Ireland. The rest of Scotland was under Macbeth, son of Findlaech, hereditary ruler of Moray. Macbeth had been commander of the forces of Duncan, King of Scots, whom he murdered in 1040. In 1057, Malcolm Canmore, son of the murdered Duncan, avenged his father's death by killing Macbeth at Lumphanan and ascending the throne. Thornfinn also died that year and, by marrying Thornfinn's widow, Ingibiorg, a native of Galloway, Malcolm brought many of the Norse controlled districts, including Galloway, under the suzerainty of the Scottish crown.

At the Battle of Hastings in 1066 William the Bastard, Duke of Normandy, a descendant of Norse settlers in France, commenced the Norman conquest of England, and thus indirectly initiated the spread of the feudal system in Scotland. The resistance this system incurred in Galloway was to impoverish the area for centuries due to continual warfare. At this time Galloway was a powerful area, which, in addition to the present countries of Kirkcudbright and Wigtown, included the whole of Ayrshire, Renfrewshire and Lanarkshire and stretched to the forest of Selkirk in the East. The culture of Galloway was Celtic, the language Gaelic and the law the Brehon law. The first Earl of Galloway to be actually 'appointed' by a Scottish monarch was David (youngest son of Malcolm Canmore) who succeeded to the Scottish throne in 1124. David was determined to be a feudal king in the Norman style. One of his first actions, therefore, was to give the whole of Annandale to a Norman Baron Robert de Brus (Bruce). Greatest of the Pictish Lords of Galloway was Fergus, who looked on such Norman acquisitions with dismay. Fergus was a great Baron in his own right, as well as being son-in-law to Henry I of England. Like his erstwhile friend David, he was a founder of many churches and monasteries. In 1130, however, he allied himself with the Earl of Moray and rose with the Galloway Cruthin against the King and his Norman supporters. But the rebellion was crushed, Moray killed and Fergus was forced to take sanctuary in Holyrood Abbey, David's own foundation in Edinburgh.

In 1135, Henry I of England died leaving the throne to his daughter Matilda, who was David's niece. When Matilda's cousin Stephen usurped the English throne, with the aid of the Anglo-Norman nobles, David invaded Northumbria to help Matilda. But the Northern English rallied under a magnificent old warrior named Thurstan, Archbishop of York and he sent them, duly absolved and blessed, to erect a Standard on Culton Moor, near Northallerton. At the battle of the Standard (1138) the Scottish King David had under his command "an army of Normans, Germans, English, of Northumbrians and Cumbrians, of men of Teviotdale and Lothian, of Picts who are commonly called Galwegians and of Scots" according to an English chronicler. The Scottish army was defeated mainly because the Galwegians insisted on the privilege given to them by Kenneth Mac Alpin of fighting in the vanguard of the Scottish Army. It is a remarkable fact that the Galwegians were taunted by English shouts of "Irish, Irish" as they joined battle.

By this time the Airgiallan Uí Thuirtri had advanced so far into Antrim that their king, O'Flynn, was styling himself 'King of Dál n Araidi'. In 1148 Muirchertach Mac Loughlin of the dominant O'Neills of Tyrone renewed his grandfather's policy of dividing Old Ulidia between four tigernai who were mere 'lords' and not 'kings'. This so alarmed his powerful vassal, Donnchad O'Carrol of Airgialla, that he was obliged to reinstate Cu Ulad Mac Donleavy as King of the Dál Fiatach. In Galloway David had magnanimously restored to Fergus the title of Governor of Galloway but by 1150 had removed most of Lanarkshire and Renfrewshire from the Earldom. When David died in 1153 and was succeeded by Malcolm IV, a boy of ten years, Fergus and his Cruthin rose again in rebellion. Malcolm's army was repulsed twice by Fergus but eventually overpowered him in 1160 and forced him to hand over his lands to his two sons, Uchtred and Gilbert. Fergus then re-entered Holyrood where he died in 1611, they say, of a broken heart. In 1165 O'Carroll of Airgialla acted again as a peace-maker between Muirchertach, who was now high-king, and Eochaid, the son and successor of Cu Ulad. Because of this he was awarded the lands of the old Cruthinic allies the Manaig (Manapii) and the Uí Bairrche (Brigantes), which were called Benna Bairrche. These lands were given to the Airgiallan Mugdorna who migrated there from O'Carroll's lands in Monaghan. This people (Mac Mahons) gave their name to the area, first in the form of Mocorne, then Morna and finally Mourne. Thus ended the last power of the Brigantes and the magnificent Manapii.

In 1166 Mac Loughlin treacherously blinded Eochaid, thus incurring the displeasure of the Church and setting the seal on his own downfall. With his death that year, O'Carroll transferred his allegiance to Rory O'Connor, King of Connacht. The Mac Donleavy thus still remained 'rex Hibernicorum Ulidiae' or 'King of Ulster'. Events were proceeding apace for also in 1166 Dermot (Diarmait) Mac Murchada, deposed King of the Lagin, faced with an alliance of Rory O'Connor and the violent Tiernan O'Rourke against him, fled to England and then to Acquitaine to seek the help of Henry II. Strengthened by the support of the Church and Henry's Exchequer, Dermot returned to Ireland the following year and made terms with his enemies. This allowed him to call over Fitzstephen and then Fitzgerald, whose company constituted the vanguard of the Anglo-Norman invasion of Ireland. Such Anglo-Norman families as the Fitzgeralds were to become more 'Irish' than the 'Irish' themselves. Dermot was again instituted as King of the Lagin, the area in which they lived having now taken the Scandinavian form Leinster. The main invasion proceeded with the arrival of Strongbow (Richard de Clare, Earl of Pembroke) on 23 August 1170 at Waterford. Although we have retained the usual epithet, 'Anglo-Norman', applied to this invasion, it should be remembered that the Norman conquest of England and Wales was a relatively recent one. This was also the age of influence of that extraordinary Norman propaganda work *Historia Regum Britanniae* (*History of the Kings of Britain*) by Galfridus Monemutensis (Geoffrey de Monmouth). The Norman French had many Bretons among them whose heritage was identical with the Welsh among whom they settled. In actuality, therefore, Strongbow's force was a Cambro-Norman one, and far from 'English' in culture, language or composition.

Following the death of Fergus, Lord of the Cruthin of Galloway, his dominion passed to his sons, Uchtred and Gilbert, according to the Celtic Law. Uchtred inherited the estates of the east in Kirkcudbrightshire and Gilbert the Western estates of Wigtownshire. Uchtred was therefore more open to the new Norman influence, and during this time mote and bailey castles were constructed in the east. Gilbert maintained an inborn hatred of the Normans, whom he saw as a threat to the ancient independence of his people. Both lords, however, owed obedience to the Kings of Scotland and in 1174 followed William the Lion on his invasion of England. But they no sooner saw him taken captive by chance by the English at Alnwick Castle than they returned with the Cruthin to Galloway, broke out into insurrection, attacked and demolished the royal castles and slaughtered all the Anglo-Normans ('the Englishmen and French') who had settled among their mountains. Later that year Gilbert quarrelled with Uchtred, captured him near Portpatrick and inflicted on him a horrible death. He then belatedly tried to strengthen his position by offering tribute to Henry II of England, but Henry declined and released William, who, by the Treaty of Falaise, became his vassal. William proceeded to invade Galloway, subdued Gilbert and attempted to purchase his peacefulness of conduct by giving him full possession of Carrick in Ayrshire. For the next ten years, however, Gilbert fought the Norman barons of Eastern Galloway and, by playing off the two kings against one another maintained that independence he so desired.

Towards the end of January 1177 John de Courcy erupted into Old Ulidia, and over the next few years made himself Master of Ulster (princeps Ultoniae). Although he owed fealty to Henry II of England, this title was purely of de Courcy's own making and Mac Donleavy was still officially 'rex Ulidiae'. De Courcy's greatest achievements were the establishment of two fine castles, Carrickfergus and Dundrum. At first strongly opposed by the Ulidians under Mac Donleavy, de Courcy's government was soon seen by them to offer some degree of protection against the O'Neills. In 1811 the Clan Owen "gained a battle over the Ulidians, and over Ui Tuirtri, and over Fir-Li around Rory Mac Donleavy and Cumee O'Flynn". Increasing raids by the Clan Owen in which they "took many thousands of cows" forced the Ulidians to appeal to de Courcy for help. And so, when the Devlins and their kin made their next raid in 1182, they were met and defeated by de Courcy in alliance with the Ulidians. At the height of his power in 1185 de Courcy was created Justiciar of Ireland and accordingly transferred the scene of his activities from Dun (Downpatrick) to Ath-Cliath (Dublin).

With the death of Gilbert that year, Roland, son of the murdered Uchtred, claimed the Lordship of Galloway. Roland had spent the previous ten years at the Scottish court, and had married the daughter of Richard de Morville, the Hereditary Constable of Scotland. He had thus become "a Scoto-Norman more than a Galwegian". Although his title was upheld by William the Lion, Gilbert's son Duncan also had a strong party in his favour and in consequence Galloway was convulsed in that civil war from which Roland emerged the victor. But Henry of England called him to order and marched north in support of Duncan. The result was a compromise by which Duncan was created Earl of Carrick, and Roland, although confirmed Lord of Galloway, was forced to swear fealty to the throne of England. In 1196, when he was appointed Constable of Scotland, Roland's influence was complete and Galloway was fast becoming a feudal state.

Meanwhile in Ulster, de Courcy's followers, including the last remnant of the Cruthin, the Iveagh, continued to harass the O'Neills and their dependants the Airgialla (Oriel). In 1197 John's brother, Jordan de Courcy, was killed by one of his own Irish retainers. This incensed and embittered John, who avenged the murder on some of the local chiefs and gave parts of their land to Duncan of Carrick, who aided him. In 1200 Roland died and was succeeded by Alan the Great, last and most powerful of the Pictish Lords of Galloway. Alan was later to expand what we may designate with hindsight as the First Return of the Cruthin to Ulster. The day was long past when the history of Ireland and Scotland was simply a matter of 'Gall' versus 'Gael'. De Courcy's independent rule in Ulster now aroused the jealousy of Hugh de Lacy, who misrepresented the Master of Ulster to the new King John of England. Following this de Courcy fell into disfavour, and was defeated by de Lacy at Downpatrick. Finally on 29 May 1205, King John granted de Lacy all of de Courcy's lands and created him Earl of Ulster. De Lacy and his half-brother Walter soon showed John that he had mistaken his men, for by 1208 they were at war with 'the English of Munster', and proved more insubordinate than 'the Irish' themselves. The final straw was their harbouring of William de Braose, whom the King hated. Consequently John called his vassals to arms.

On 20 June 1210, King John and his army landed at Waterford. There they were joined by the Justiciar, de Gray and an Irish contingent. John was notably accompanied by John de Courcy and Alan the Great. De Lacy fled to Ulster, first to Dundrum and finally to Carrickfergus. At this point King John secured the services of Hugh O'Neill to assist in expelling de Lacy, and O'Neill, having done what was required of him, left the scene without submitting hostages to the King. This rebuff John was not to forgive. Hugh de Lacy and William de Braose escaped to Scotland but the latter's wife and their two sons were captured by Duncan of Carrick. For his service Duncan was granted lands in Antrim. Then in 1212, representing Alan, Duncan was assigned by King John the whole north-east of the Province from the Glens of Antrim to the River Foyle. In that year also, Thomas Mac Uchtry (Alan's brother and earl of Atholl) gained that part of Derry which belonged to the O'Neill. The main Cruthinic (ie 'Scottish') settlement which followed appears to have been around Coleraine. The power of the Galwegians at this time is exemplified by the presence of Alan among the Barons of England at Runnymede in 1215 when King John was forced to sign the *Magna Carta*.

Yet, whatever may have been his faults, John showed leniency during the last year of his reign and Walter de Lacy, on payment of a fine, had restored to him his possessions in Ulster. Meanwhile Alan's power grew with his navy. For several years following 1220 he led it against the Norse of the Western Isles and Isle of Man. Olaf, King of Man then found it necessary to appeal to Haco, King of Norway for protection. When Alan heard news of this he also sent a message to Norway stating that the sea was as navigable between Scotland and Norway as between Norway and Scotland, and politely expressed the hope that he might prove that Norwegian harbours were as accessible as those of Galloway. Haco replied by ordering the assembly of 80 Norse ships at the Orkneys, which, under Olaf, sailed towards Man. Not to be outdone, Alan raised his whole Navy of 150 ships, much to Olaf's despair, so that the erstwhile King of Man turned and fled to the North. But John's grant to Alan in Antrim was resented bitterly by the de Lacy's. In 1222 the son of Hugh de Lacy came to Ireland and joined Hugh O'Neill. Together they destroyed the Galwegian castle of Coleraine. When Hugh de Lacy was restored to the Earldom of Ulster in 1226–27 the lands of Alan and Thomas of Galloway were exempted from his grant, but his feud with them continued unabated. At length, in 1234, Alan died, last in the male line of the Mac Uchtrys, last of the native Lords of Galloway, and he was buried with due ceremony at Dundrennan Abbey.

Alan left three daughters, Helena, Christina and Dervorgilla, each of whom was married to an Anglo-Norman noble. Helena was married to Roger de Quency, Earl of Winchester; Christina to William de Fortibus, Earl of Albemarle; and Dervorgilla to John Balliol of Barnard Castle, near Durham. Dervorgilla the Good was one of the finest women of her age, but she had to reckon with Gaelic male chauvinism enshrined in the Brehon law of Galloway, by which no female could inherit land or exercise government. The Galwegians resented the introduction of alien lords and demanded that the Lordship should be assumed by the Crown. When this request was denied they rose in rebellion in support of Alan's illegitimate son Thomas. But Alexander II enforced the natural rights of the three women and crushed the rebellion. By doing so he strengthened the feudal institutions, with the introduction of rules governing the granting of charters for the holding of lands, the leasing of such land from landowners to tenants, the security of property and the advancement of agriculture.

In 1242, Patrick, son of Thomas of Galloway, was murdered. Walter Bissett and his nephew John were accused of the crime and outlawed in Scotland. They fled to Ulster were they were granted by de Lacy land around Glenarm and elsewhere in Antrim previously held by the Galloway nobles. In that year say the *Annals of Ulster*, "Hugh de Lacy, Earl of Ulster rested", and he like his late enemy Alan, left no male heirs. The Bissett lands also passed eventually to a girl. This sole heiress was Mairi Bissett, and through marriage to Mac Donnell, Lord of the Isles, the Glens of Antrim were to receive an unending stream of 'Scots', who were mainly of Norse-Airgiallan descent.

When Christina of Galloway died in 1245 her estates were divided between her surviving sisters, whose husbands thus shared the Lordship of Galloway. Later that year Alexandra Comyn, Earl of Buchan, succeeded de Quincy in right of his wife and introduced to the district the important office of Justiciary. Balliol and Dervorgilla remained one of the wealthiest couples of their time, and soon became popular in Galloway through their gifts to the Church and the poor. Balliol also founded a hostel for students at Oxford and Dervorgilla is renowned for building and endowing that famous College which bears her husband's name on the site of this foundation. Mainly due to their influence therefore, Galloway at last accepted the Normans as a fact of life.

But there was no Dervorgilla in Ulster. As well as continued Gaelic resistance to the Anglo-Normans, there was constant warfare between the O'Donnells of Tirconnell and the O'Neills of Tirowen. In 1258 a conference was held to promote a spirit of unity among the Gaelic chiefs. At this gathering Brian O'Neill was elected 'high-king', although important figures such as Donald Oge O'Donnell refused to acknowledge him. One result, however, was the forging of an alliance between Brian O'Neill and Felim O'Connor, King of Connacht. This alliance was crushed by 'the English' at the battle of Downpatrick which ensued in 1260. The Iveagh Cruthin and the Ulaid refused to join the O'Neills at this battle. Sweet indeed was their revenge for the burning of their old capital of Emania, and continued Gaelic aggression for nearly a thousand years. Yet even in the midst of Anglo-Norman expansion, the O'Neills coveted each other's property. In 1275 the Tirowen (Tyrone) families invaded Tirconnell and devastated the entire district. Following this incursion they were pursued by O'Donnell of Tirconnell and defeated "with the loss of men, horses, accoutrements, arms and armour." In 1283 the positions were reversed and it was the turn of Tirconnell to be heavily defeated by O'Neill of Tirowen. The 'English' of the North were now led by Richard de Burgh, the 'Red Earl of Ulster'. Richard's father Walter had inherited the de Lacy territory by right of his wife, who was the daughter of Hugh de Lacy. And so, in 1286 we find Richard compelling the submission of the O'Donnell. He also deposed the O'Neill of Tyrone for a time, and in 1290 again plundered Tirconnell. Later he planted a colony in Inishowen and erected a castle at Moville to command the whole district.

The accidental death of the great Scottish King Alexander III, conqueror of Haco of Norway and the Norse of the Western Isles, left his little grand-daughter, the Maid of Norway, as the new Queen of Scotland. This little Queen was the only child of the marriage of Alexander's daughter Margaret and Eric, King of Norway. A treaty was made with Edward I of England, whereby she should marry his son, Prince Edward. In 1290, however, she died at the Orkneys on her way to Scotland from Norway. With her death commenced the Wars of Succession in Scotland. There were 13 claimants to the throne and Edward I was requested to adjudicate between the main two Scoto-Norman nobles. These were John, son of Balliol and Dervorgilla, and Robert de Bruce, Lord of Annadale and Cleveland. Both were descendants of David, Earl of Huntingdon, brother of William the Lion. John Balliol claimed as the grandson of David's eldest daughter Margaret, wife of Alan the Great of Galloway; Robert de Bruce as the son of David's second daughter, wife of the Lord of Annadale. Before judgement Edward made the claimants swear to maintain him as their liege lord. Edward was subsequently to choose the weak Balliol as king, the judgement being in favour of primogeniture, and so, on 30 November 1292, John Balliol was crowned at Scone.

In the events which followed the Galwegians naturally sided with the Comyns and Balliols, and accordingly shared in their disasters. It soon became apparent that when Balliol surrendered his claim to independent jurisdiction in Scotland, with the resultant adjudication by the English Court on the rights of Scots, Edward would waste no time in manoeuvring the subjection of the country. In order to pre-empt this, the Scots allied with France, with whom Edward was at war, and in 1295 invaded England. However, they were repulsed at Carlisle. Edward left his French campaign under truce, returned home, marched North and stormed Berwick. The English forces won a further victory at Dunbar, and aided by the Ulidian forces of the Earl of Ulster, soon received the submission of all the fortifications of Scotland. Balliol, 'King Empty Jacket', was ignominiously forced to surrender his crown, his country, and his personal honour at Brechin. Edward now considered Galloway specifically as his own, and appointed over it a governor, Henry de Percy, who obliged the sheriffs and Bailiffs to account for the profits and rents of their bailiwicks at the Royal Exchequer in Berwick.

Then there arose among the Scots a great guerrilla leader. William Wallace's area of origin was Renfrewshire in Old Strathclyde, but his family came from Oswestry on the Welsh border and the name Wallace means 'Welshman' in its broad sense, as from the Old British lands stretching from Strathclyde, Aeron (Ayrshire), Galloway, Cumbria, Lancashire, Wales, Cornwall and Brittany, thus indicating a Brittonic heritage. Wallace, in 1279, at only 25 years of age, defeated a large English force under Cressingham and Surrey at the Battle of Stirling, freed the Scottish Realm and assumed the title of governor. In 1298 Wallace marched into the west "to chastise the men of Galloway, who had espoused the party of the Comyns and supported the pretensions of the English." He was defeated, nevertheless, by Edward I at the Battle of Falkirk on 22 July that year. During a further campaign in 1300, Edward I marched from Carlisle through Dumfriesshire into Galloway, and overran the whole of the Low Country from the Nith to the Cree, while a detachment pushed into Wigtownshire. Wallace was finally captured and brought to London, where in 1305, he was hung, drawn and quartered.

The leadership of the Scottish patriots was taken up by the Norman nobleman Robert the Bruce, grandson of that Robert de Bruce we have already met, and son of Marjory of Carrick, grand-daughter of Duncan. Thus Bruce was a Scoto-Norman. During the early part of the War of Independence, like many such Barons with conflicting interests, his loyalties had wavered between Wallace and the English King, for he had immense estates in England. With the death of the brave Wallace, Bruce saw that he was first and foremost a Scot, and entered into a conspiracy with John 'The Red' Comyn, Balliol's nephew by marriage. Comyn's betrayal of Bruce to Edward cast the die for Bruce, and when he slew Comyn before the altar of the Church of the Friars Minor in Dumfries (10 February 1306), the resultant alienation of the Galwegians and the Pope made his task a more difficult one than ever. Bruce was forced to hasten on to Glasgow, collecting such notable adherents as Sir James Douglas on the way, and then to Scone, where on 27 March 1306, he was crowned King of Scots by the Bishop of St Andrews.

Bruce's fight for the kingdom itself was to be an onerous one, and dogged by personal tragedy. A defeat by the English army at Methven (19 June 1306) was followed by another at Strathfillan (11 August). By killing the Red Comyn Bruce had not only alienated the Galwegians, but had made a deadly and brave enemy in John of Lorn, the Comyn's uncle, and a great Highland chief. After being hounded through the Highlands, he sailed to the refuge of Rathlin Island, north of Antrim, where he spent part of the winter of 1306. Rathlin was owned at this time by Angus Oge Mac Donnell. In the meantime Robert's wife, his daughter and his sisters were taken captive by the English; his brother-in-law Sir Christopher Seton, Sir Simon Frazer and several of his closest friends were put to death. In early February 1307 his two brothers Alexander and Thomas disembarked with a small force at Loch Ryan, but were captured by the Galwegians under the Mac Dowells, handed over to Edward I and subsequently hanged. Bruce himself landed on the Carrick coast in the Spring, now supported by the northern O'Neills. The further adventures of this famous king belong as much to Romance as to History, particularly his unhappy sojourn in the Galloway Hills. The whole aspect of the situation was changed by the death of Edward I at Burgh-on-Sands on the Solway on 7 June 1307, and the accession of the weak Edward II.

The subjugation of Buchan which then took place in 1308 saw vast areas of Buchan in north-east Scotland, then ruled by Clan Comyn, burned to the ground by Bruce and his ruthless brother Edward, immediately following their May 1308 defeat of John Comyn, Earl of Buchan, at the Battle of Barra. Bruce's men then proceeded to kill those loyal to the Comyns (men, women and children) in an orgy of ethnic cleansing, destroying their homes, farms, crops and slaughtering their cattle. This was to haunt Bruce on his deathbed but by terrorising the locals he prevented any possible chance of future hostility towards him and his men. The Comyns had ruled Buchan for nearly a century, from 1214, when William Comyn inherited the title from his wife. Such was the terror and destruction, however, that the people of Buchan lost all loyalties to the Comyns and never again rose against Bruce's supporters. Galloway was overrun by Robert's brother, Edward the Bruce, and a last stand was made by a combined force of Isles men and Galwegians somewhere in the Valley of the Dee on 29 June 1308. Robert accordingly made Edward Lord of Galloway for his services, the success of which may be gauged by the fact that in this area only Buittle and Dumfries remained under English control. By the close of 1313 Berwick and Stirling alone in the whole of Scotland were still English and the independence of Scotland was finally assured by the ever-memorable Battle of Bannockburn on 24 June 1314. Truly Bruce was a Summer, not a Winter King, as his wife was said to have prophesied.

The natural extension of the victory of Scottish independence was the invitation of O'Neill of Tyrone to Robert I offering to make Edward King of Ireland. Robert accepted readily, for the fierce ambition of this brother was a threat to the King of Scots himself. And so, on 25 May 1315, Edward Bruce landed at Larne Harbour on the Antrim Coast. He was joined by Robert Bissett with the Scots of Antrim and by Donald O'Neill, son of Brian of Tyrone. In spite of his age, Richard, the Red Earl of Ulster, assembled his retainers in Roscommon and marched to Athlone, where he was joined by Felim O'Connor and the army of Connacht. The 'English' army then marched into Ulster, laying waste the country of the O'Neill. Meanwhile Bruce had overrun Down and Louth, laying waste old Ulidia, destroying the 'English' and their Ulidian support. Then according to the *Annals of Clonmacnoise*:

"by the procurement of O'Neale and Ulstermen he took his journey to Cowllerayne [Coleraine] of the North and to the borders of Innisowen, and fell down and broke the bridge of Cowllerayne to stop the Earl's passage over the river of Bann, whom the Earl followed until he came to the same river, and from thence thro' Ulster, where he marched holding on their course of spoyleing and destroying all places where they came."

Both armies then faced each other across the troubled waters of the bridgeless Bann. At this point O'Connor deserted the Red Earl, who was thus forced to retreat and subsequently defeated in a battle at Connor near Ballymena on 10 September 1315. Following a campaign of devastation, Edward was eventually crowned King of Ireland on 1 May 1316, in the presence of a large assembly of Irish and Scottish nobles. That Autumn King Robert I sailed from Galloway with a force to help his brother, but withdrew the following year. Edward was finally defeated by an 'English' force under John de Birmingham at Faughart near Dundalk in 1318. Edward was killed in this battle and with the death of this cruelly ambitious but exceptionally brave Lord of Galloway, the Scottish invasion came to an end.

Now the Pope was a powerful political figure in medieval times. Bruce's killing of Comyn (Cummings) on holy ground at Greyfriars Kirk led to his excommunication. The Pope had turned his back on Bruce, so that in 1318 Bruce, his lieutenants and his bishops were all excommunicated. Bruce reacted by having three letters sent to the Pope. The first was a letter from himself, the second from the Scots clergy, and the third from the nobles of Scotland. The third letter became known as the 'Declaration of Arbroath' and survives to this day, being used by modern Scottish Nationalists for political purposes. In this letter, the Scots, who claimed descent from Irish invader warlords, vaunted their expulsion of the native Britons and their utter destruction of the Picts, neither of which they were actually able to achieve, for we are the descendants of these ancient peoples.

But the power of the Earls of Ulster was crushed. The Red Earl was imprisoned in Dublin because his daughter was the wife of Robert the Bruce. Humiliated and grieved, he retired to a monastery where he died in 1326. The devastation in Ulster was followed by famine and famine was followed by disease. The earldom passed to Richard's grandson, William 'The Brown Earl'. William lacked his grandfather's qualities as well as his power and was inevitably murdered near Belfast in 1333. All over Ulster the Anglo-Normans gaelicised themselves to survive; the de Burgh's adopted the name Burke, the de Mandevilles became the McQuillans, Lords of the Route (Dalriata). Only in Dublin and its Pale did the 'English' government keep control. Meanwhile, with the death of Robert the Bruce, Galloway again became the theatre of domestic war. In 1334, aided and accompanied by Edward III of England, Edward Balliol renewed the pretensions of his father by invading Scotland. In 1346 David II, son of the Bruce, was defeated and captured at the Battle of Durham, and Balliol again ruled over his patrimonial estates from Buittle Castle. Balliol was also nominally 'King' of Scotland until 1353 when Sir William Douglas invaded Kircudbrightshire, compelled the McDowalls and McCulloughs, hereditary enemies of the Bruces, to change sides, and expelled Balliol. From this time on these Cruthinic families never again were subject to the domination of England and only as 'British' were they later ruled by a Parliament in London.

Even under de Courcy and the Earls of Ulster Mac Donleavy had remained 'rex Hibernicorum Ulidiae', King of Ulster. With the destruction of the Anglo-Normans, a branch of the Tyrone O'Neills, the Clan of Yellow-haired Hugh, Clann Aedha Bhuidhe (Clannaboy, Clandeboye) moved into Antrim and North Down, anciently Trian Congaill, the Third of Congal Claen. Of the Old Ulidians only the Mac Aonghusa (Mac Guinness, Mac Genis, Magennis, Mac Innes, Ennis) retained any power. This family were chiefs of the Iveagh Cruthin, the other surviving families of whom were the Mac Artain (Macarton, McCartan, Carton), O Ruanaidh (Rooney, Roney), O Labhradha (Lowry, Armstrong, Lavery) and O Sluaghain (Sloan). The Dál Fiatach (Ulaid) were powerless, but such important families as the Irvines, Mac Veighs, Nevins and Mac Donleavys (Livingstones) survived. All these families now owned allegiance to O'Neill. Yet it was not until 1364 that Hugh O'Neill of Tyrone is styled "ri Uladh, rex Ulidiae" by the *Annals of Ulster*. Then and only then was the name Ulidia, Ulaidh, Ulster applied again to the whole North; the Gaelic O'Neill conquest of Ulster complete; and the kingdom of Old Ulidia destroyed forever.

The empty title of the Earl of Ulster was inherited by Lionel, Duke of Clarence, who had married the only daughter and heiress of the Brown Earl. Lionel was created Lord Lieutenant of Ireland by his father Edward III, but could make no headway against either the 'Irish' or 'English' of Ireland outside the Pale. In 1367 he summoned a Parliament to pass the Statute of Kilkenny, which attempted to maintain a separation of 'Irish' from 'English' by making the adoption of Gaelic customs, language and dress by the newer inhabitants criminal offences. The 'English' government, however, was so weak that the provisions of the Statute were but partially and spasmodically enforced. The O'Neills were triumphant, but only in 1381 could Niall O'Neill legitimise his claim to Ulster in the eyes of the learned classes at a feast he held for them near Emain Macha (Emania). By this time the whole of Galloway was reunited under the feudal Lordship of the famous Douglas, Archibald the Grim. Yet the Celtic Law of Galloway survived until at least 1384, even though continued war with England was uniting the various ethnic groups of Southern Scotland into patriotic 'Border Scots'. In 1388 Archibald became the most powerful subject of Scotland when he inherited the great honours and original estates of the House of Douglas following the death of the celebrated Sir James Douglas at the Battle of Otterburn (Chevy Chase). And so, subject to the withering influences of the 'Irish' O'Neill in Ulster and the 'Scottish' Douglas in Galloway, the memory of the Cruthin flickered, grew dim and almost died.

CHAPTER 5

THE BRITISH AND THE AMERICANS

URING THE FIFTEEN AND sixteenth centuries the Galwegians, although culturally 'Celtic' became classified together with the peoples of Strathclyde, Lothian and the East under the label of 'Lowland Scots'. The emergence of a strictly 'Highland' society as opposed to a 'Lowland' one can only be dated as late as the fourteenth century. The social differences were originally only of emphasis; in the 'Highlands' kinship was modified by feudalism and in the 'Lowlands' feudalism was modified by kinship. Cultural differences were more profound, based firstly on the gradual extinction of Gaelic even in Galloway and its survival in the North and West, and secondly on the formation of royal burghs in the Lowlands and the establishment of a 'Middle Class' of merchants and tradesmen. Yet, contrary to popular belief, the Clan 'system' remained strong in the Borders well into the seventeenth century. A more important factor was the growth of Protestantism in Europe and the rise of Calvinism in Scotland. In 1560 the Scottish Parliament and reformation General Assembly abolished the Papal authority and allowed the eventual establishment of the Presbyterian Church of Scotland. Only in Scandinavia was the Protestant take-over accompanied by less bad feeling and there was none of that butchery so marked in the England of Henry VIII, Mary and Elizabeth. To all intents and purposes, then, the Galloway Cruthin settled down as Presbyterian Lowland Scots.

In Ulster at this time Arthur Magennis was Bishop of Dromore and his kinsman Eugene Magennis was Bishop of Down. It is generally assumed that, whatever may have been their theological views, both bishops accepted the Reformation Settlement under Elizabeth and conformed to its requirements. These requirements, however, were not rigidly enforced, even in Dublin and the Pale. Elizabeth's policy for Ireland was not motivated by missionary zeal but by concern for the safety of England itself from Spain. Now Ulster was the most Gaelic Province of Ireland and the fear of its eventual anglicisation provoked an insurrection by Hugh O'Neill of Tyrone in 1595. The War that followed was a cruel and bloody one, which left large areas of Ulster virtually without inhabitants. Antrim and Down, however, already consisted for the most part of woodlands, marsh and bogland according to the contemporary Camden. The only part of the two countries not represented as 'waste' were the southern part of the Ards Peninsula, the Barony of Lecale, and the Kingdom of Mourne, which were controlled by people of mainly Anglo-Norman descent, eg Audleys, Savages and Whites. The Iveagh Cruthin, as represented by Sir Hugh Magennis, remained consistently loyal to Elizabeth and were described as her only friends in Ulster. On 24 March 1602 Hugh O'Neill submitted to Mountjoy as her Deputy, not knowing that the greatest of Queens had died six days earlier.

Thus was the stage set for what I would call the Second Return of the Cruthin, the Great Return. By the end of the sixteenth century Scots settlers were already migrating to Antrim. Among these was the son of Sir Alexander MacNaughten, killed at Flodden. The Clan Nechtan or MacNaughten were the descendants of the Pictish Kings, and the name is commemorated by that victory which Brude, King of the Picts, won in AD 685 at Nechtansmere against the invading Northumbrian Angles. The line of chiefs of this most ancient of tribes is now represented by the MacNaughtens of Dunderave. In 1605 and 1606 settlement of Down and Antrim became the official policy of James I, first King of Scotland and England combined, and Old Ulidia became virtually an extension of the Scottish Lowlands. The success of this policy resulted in the Plantation of Ulster in 1610. This was less effective and included only six counties; namely Cavan, Donegal, Fermanagh, Tyrone, Armagh and Londonderry. Ironically, one of the most successful settlements was by Scottish Catholics, and Anglo-Scottish names such as Hume are still prominent among the Roman Catholic community of Western modern provincial Ulster.

But the settlers of Old Ulidia for the most part were the Lowland Scots of Galloway and Carrick, and in their hearts flowed the blood of the Cruthin. Among them were the families of MacClenaghan, MacClintock, MacClure, MacComb, MacCosh, MacCracken, MacCrea, Craig, MacCullough, MacCutcheon, Ferguson, MacIlrath, MacKee, MacMaster, Nelson and MacPeake, to name only a few. Perhaps the most interesting of such names, in that it indicates a direct original derivation from Ulster, is that of MacCullough, which is the anglicisation of Mac Con Uladh or 'Hound of Ulster'. Such families imprinted on the north-eastern corner of the island a temperament which played an important role in the creation of the Western World as we know it today. They were good and they were bad; they were cruel and they were kind; they were simple and they were strong. They were the British called Ulstermen, the Scotch-Irish, the Ulster Scots, the Picts called Galwegians, the Cruthin, but most of all they were the Ancient Kindred of Ireland.

The Great Return of the Cruthin to Ulster should be judged only in the context of contemporary events. All over the south-west of Scotland a new generation of working people was rising who were to change the face of civilisation. Using the Holy Bible as their source and inspiration, they destroyed the notion that learning was the sole prerogative of the Chosen Few and declared the greatest of all Liberties – Freedom of Thought. This in itself was bound to produce a reaction from the prevailing system of government, whose head considered himself the Divine Elect of God. James, reared under the sure and steadfast hand of the mighty Knox, had mellowed into Episcopacy and sought to re-introduce bishops into Scotland. In 1614 his favourite, William Cowper, a minister of Perth who had hitherto been thought a strict Presbyterian, became Bishop of Galloway and duly supported the *Five Articles of Perth* in 1618, which restored what was regarded by most Galwegians as sheer papistry. In 1621 the Parliament of Scotland ratified these Articles and declared that all ministers who would not conform to them should be imprisoned or banished.

By this time there were at least 8,000 settlers on the Estates of Hamilton and Montgomery in North Down alone, with at least 50,000 in the North as a whole. Although a large element of these Scots were of the old Galloway Cruthinic stock, there were also elements of Brittonic Stock from Strathclyde (eg Wallaces, Walshes and Welshes) and the other Middle British Kingdoms of the Borders of Scotland and England (eg Anderson, Armstrong, Beattie, Bell, Carlisle, Carruthers, Charlton, Crosier, Burns, Davison, Dixon, Dodds, Douglas, Dunn, Elliot, Forster, Gilchrist, Glendenning, Graham, Gray, Hall, Harden, Heron, Hetherington, Hodgson, Hume, Hunter, Jamieson, Johnstone, Kerr, Little, Lowther, Maxwell, Medford [later Mitford], Milburn, Moffat, Musgrave,

Nixon, Noble, Oliver, Potts, Reed, Robson, Routledge, Rutherford, Scott, Stokoe, Storey, Tailor, Tait, Thomson, Trotter, Turnbull [Trimble], Turner, Wilkinson and Young).

There were smaller elements of Norse, 'Norman' who were actually French, Anglo-Saxon, Dalriadan and Pictish stock as well. Fewer families came from the countries around Edinburgh (the Lothians and Berwick), and were thus of mixed Anglo-Saxon and Brittonic origins. Lastly, the smallest contingent came from the district lying between Aberdeen and Inverness in the north-east, and were of mixed Dalriadan and Pictish stock. Furthermore those 'English' settlers planted by the Puritan Lord Deputy Sir Arthur Chichester were mostly from Lancashire, Cheshire and Devon (Old Domnonia), and thus basically of Brittonic Stock. The third element consisted of Londoners, 12 Companies of whom were given most of the county of Coleraine, whose name they changed to Londonderry. Most of them did not find the area to their liking, and soon returned to London.

Scottish, actually British, influence was therefore predominant throughout the north and east of provincial Ulster, and it was natural that Presbyterians such as Robert Blair should take refuge there. Blair settled in Bangor in 1623, having been forced by the rise of Episcopacy to resign his professional chair in the college at Glasgow. On the other hand, for some 20 years after the Plantation of Ulster, the Protestant Church in Ireland was one and undivided, and three-quarters of its people in Ulster were Scottish Presbyterians. It is difficult to ascertain just how many of the Iveagh Cruthin accepted the concept of Calvinism. Those who did so 'anglicised' their names to become Cartons, Lowrys and Maginnises. More, however, with the names of Macartan, Lavery and Maguinness will be found in the records of the Church of Ireland (Old Catholic) Diocese of Dromore. Many others retained the Roman Catholic religion, as did many 'Gaels' of Tyrone and Tirconnell and others of the Mid-Ulster Airgiallans, the 'Scottish Highlanders' of Antrim (Norse-Airgiallans) eg the MacDonnells and MacSparrans, and the Cambro-Norman Irish eg the MacQuillans and Fitzgeralds, the latter of whom, of course, have been astonishingly critical of 'English involvement in Ireland'. As for the Ulaid, the old aristocracy of Down, families such as the Irvines, Nevins, Kearneys and Livingstones (Mac Donleavy) became prominent among those who profess the Presbyterian faith in particular and the Protestant faith in general. In summary, therefore, we may generalise that there was concentrated into the north-east of Ulster the most ancient population groups of Europe, very largely Protestant in religion, non-feudal in society and pre-Gaelic in ethnic origin. The majority were descended from the Pretani, the 'People of the Cruthin'. These ancient peoples are known in their future history as the British called Ulstermen, and under this name they enter the stage of modern history.

It was to be primarily the religious differences which were to shape the allegiances of these descendants of the Cruthin as a whole in the following centuries. Wars of Religion were now raging all over Europe, and the Rhineland in particular was suffering the devastation of the Thirty Year's War. Roman Catholic reaction was centred on the Hapsburg Dynasty, first as rulers of Spain and then as rulers of Austria and the Holy Roman Empire. Scandinavia and the North German States were bulwarks of Protestantism, and for the present France's large Huguenot population was protected by the benign Edict of Nantes. It was thus natural that the Roman Catholic Irish should look towards Southern Europe for support. It was just as natural for the Protestant Irish to fear such support and seek to destroy it. But sermons on morality should not enter into the discussion, since each side suffered as much as the other. Neither should there be used such valueless terms as 'native' Irish for the pre-Norman inhabitants of Ireland and 'Old English' for the Cambro-Normans, for these belong solely to the propaganda works of their own generations. The important result, as far as the children of the Cruthin were concerned, was that the rise of Protestantism led to a political fusion of the Roman Catholic recusants of Ireland, and a mutual antagonism between sections of the descendants of the Cruthin which has lasted until this day.

The accession of Charles I in 1625 allowed Roman Catholics to negotiate concessions ('Graces') concerning such questions as land tenure and religion, in return for an annual payment to the King's Exchequer. No family could be dispossessed if it had held its lands for more than 60 years. The Oath of Supremacy was replaced by a simple oath of allegiance for those Roman Catholics seeking to practise law, and was not now essential as a prerequisite for wards of court to come into their inheritance. In 1633 Charles I made Thomas Wentworth Lord Deputy of Ireland and William Laud became

Archbishop of Canterbury. Both men were to cause sore affliction to fall on the Presbyterian people of Ulster. Under Laud's High Church influence a convocation of the Church of Ireland at length accepted the *Thirty-nine Articles* of the Church of England. A loyal vassal of his Absolute Monarch, Wentworth laid down as one of his policies the religious conformity of the whole of Ireland, and strongly supported Laud's stipulations. The result was that those Ulster ministers who would not conform, such as John Livingstone of Antrim, were forced to return to Scotland. There, however, they strengthened the resistance to *Laud's Liturgy*, that 'Popish-English-Scottish-Mass-Service-Book' as it was locally described. In 1637 this resistance burst out into rebellion and resulted in the Scottish Covenant so widely accepted in Galloway. For the next five years most Scottish congregations in Ulster were without their ministers, and as many as 500 crossed the Irish Sea on one occasion to celebrate the Lord's Supper under the exiled Livingstone at Stranraer in Galloway.

In 1638 Livingstone represented Wigtownshire at the notable Glasgow meeting of the General Assembly of the Church of Scotland which abolished the Bishops, the *Articles of Perth*, the *Book of Canons* and the *Prayer Book*. Such actions were in total defiance of Charles I, and by the spring of 1639 War between the King and Covenanters was inevitable. Wentworth was determined that no such defiance would take place among the Kindred Scots of Ulster and tried to impose on them a 'Black Oath', by which they would swear to obey the King's royal commands and would declare against the Scottish rebellion. Those who refused returned to Scotland. Furthermore, when Wentworth (now Lord Strafford) learned that Charles was planning to invade Scotland in 1640, he raised an army in Ireland of 9,000 men to help the King. The majority of these were Roman Catholics. All this was anathema to the increasingly powerful Parliamentarians in England, and there was also a call to arms by the Army of the Covenant in Scotland. Opposition to Strafford grew as the power of Charles declined, and the English Parliament finally had him attainted and executed on 12 May 1641.

The opportunity offered to the Roman Catholic Irish by civil unrest in England, as well as fear engendered by the Puritan Aspect of the new English Parliament, led inevitably to Rebellion in Ireland later that year. The plans for this were worked out by a member of one of the last Cruthinic families in Southern Ireland, gaelicised more than a millennium before. The O'Mores or Moores were among the final remnants of the Loigse, who had held the territory named from them, Laois (in English form 'Leix'), a portion of the Leinster county now so named, formerly Queen's County. The Loigse had been ruled by the Moores from the earliest documentary period until they lost their lands in the English plantation of the fifteenth century. It was therefore primarily against the more recent English settlers and the Dublin government that Rory O'More directed the primary assault in October 1641. Prominent among his fellow conspirators were northern malcontents led by Sir Phelim O'Neill and with him was Sir Con Magennis of the Iveagh Cruthin. Within a few weeks the Cambro-Normans and other Anglo-Irish of the Pale joined the insurrection on the side of the rebels.

It was the declared policy of the rebels at the beginning of the uprising that the Presbyterian people (Ulster Scots) should be left alone because of their 'Gaelic' origins, but the conflict quickly became a sectarian one, and the distinction between 'English' and 'Scots' was not long maintained. It was the English settlers who suffered most, however, and several thousand lost their lives both in the fighting itself and in the privations which followed. By February 1642 only a few areas remained in the hands of the Protestants. The Ulster Scots held North Down and South Antrim, including the town of Belfast and the walled city of Carrickfergus. The towns of Coleraine, Londonderry and Enniskillen were also defended without difficulty, as was north Donegal. In the South, however, only Dublin, Drogheda, Cork and a few scattered outposts remained under government control. Sir Phelim O'Neill claimed that he was acting under Charles I's authority, and exhibited as proof a commission under the Great Seal of England. Although such a claim was undoubtedly untrue, suspicion of the King's complicity was not easily refuted in England and Scotland. In March 1642 Charles gave his assent to an Act of the English Parliament which promised any 'Adventurers', who would contribute funds for the war, repayment in confiscated Irish Land. Although most of the money so accumulated was actually used later by the Parliament to finance its war with the King himself, the Adventurers were to form an influential group in the suppression of the war and the subsequent settlement of Ireland under Cromwell.

In April 1642 the Presbyterian people were relieved by a Scottish Army under Major-General Monro, who landed at Carrickfergus. In May the Confederate Catholics met at Kilkenny, where they set up a provisional government. In June, however, Monro took the offensive and drove back the Northern Catholic forces, recapturing Newry, Mountjoy and Dungannon. Rebel hopes rose again, nevertheless, with the arrival of their natural leader, Owen Roe O'Neill, in Lough Swilly towards the end of July. Shortly afterwards Thomas Preston, an Anglo-Irish Roman Catholic leader, arrived at Waterford and was well received in the Pale. Both men had achieved military reputations in the Spanish Netherlands, and their personal rivalries highlighted the ill-concealed distrust between the Pre-Norman and Anglo-Irish factions. In August, Civil war broke out in England between King and Parliament, and the loyalties of the Protestant Parliament in Dublin were divided between the two Parties. The Confederation of Kilkenny, on the other hand, met in October 1642 and adopted the motto 'Pro Deo, pro Rege, pro Patria Hibernia unanimio', declaring, in effect, their loyalty to the King.

Following the indecisive Battle of Edgehill at the end of October, the King entered Oxford in triumph but, mindful of the Army of the Catholic Confederacy, at length in January 1643 secretly ordered his Irish representatives, Ormond and Clanricarde, to enter into negotiations with the rebels. Ormond, the 'Cavalier Duke', who was of the Butler family, was a Protestant Anglo-Irishman of Norman origins and had many relatives among the Cambro-Norman element of the rebel army. Although these Anglo-Irish Catholics were willing to reach an agreement with Ormond, the pre-Norman Irish were satisfied by the Official Papal Agent, Father Scarampi, that they could win the outright victory. Thus dissension ensued. In September 1643 a truce was finally arranged between Ormond and the Confederacy, but this was denounced outright by Monro, who subsequently signed the Solemn League and Covenant with his fellow Scots and the English Parliamentarians. The Scottish Covenanters had been waiting for such a truce ever since the Earl of Antrim was caught returning to Ireland from England with letters concerning a scheme to raise his clan, the Catholic MacDonnells (MacDonalds) of Ulster, for an invasion of Scotland on behalf of the King. They were proved right again by the uprising of the great Scottish Royalist, James Graham, Marquis of Montrose, who raised the Norse-Airgiallan Highlanders and, with a fine body of their relatives from the Isles and Ulster sent by Antrim, went from victory to victory over the Covenant. On 14 June 1645, however, the English Parliamentarians under Oliver Cromwell won the decisive battle of Naseby against Charles, and when Montrose was finally defeated at Philiphaugh, near Selkirk, in September 1645 by the Covenant Army, the power of the Cavaliers fast ebbed away. The period of the 'First Civil War' of the Three Kingdoms finally ended when Charles surrendered to the Scots on 5 May 1646.

By this time the new Papal Nuncio, John Rinnuccini, Archbishop of Fermio, was providing funds from the Vatican for the Catholic Army of Ulster under Owen Roe O'Neill. In June 1646, this trained force won a notable victory over Monro and his Scots at Benburb in County Armagh. If O'Neill had then pressed on to Carrickfergus he would have probably won Ulster. Instead he chose to remain inactive for some months, acting only when the negotiations of the Kilkenny Supreme Council with Ormond were not going to his liking. Finally, at the end of September, he marched south to Kilkenny and joining up with Preston, dissolved the Council and installed Rinnuccini as the President of a new one. Ormond continued to bargain with both Preston and Sir James Dillon of Athlone, but was thwarted for the moment by the sagacity of the superior O'Neill. Eventually he saw his best purpose was to come to terms with Michael Jones, the Parliamentary commander in Ireland, so he handed over Dublin to Jones, returned to England and reported to the King, who was by now a prisoner of the English Parliament.

Time was running out for Charles, who at last decided to play his King of Scots card with the Covenanters for, whatever his religious or political beliefs, he was a Stuart. Under the influence of the more moderate Covenanters ('Engagers') led by the Duke of Hamilton, the Scottish Army, which included several of Munro's Ulster regiments, invaded England and were utterly defeated by the New Model Army under Cromwell at Preston early in 1648. This re-opening of the Civil War, or Second Civil War as it is sometimes called, caused a complete change of allegiances in Ulster. Ormond considered that the time was now ripe for him to return again to Ireland for, with the disaffection of Inchiquin, Lord President of Munster, as well as the Scots, from the parliamentary side, and the support of the

Roman Catholic Anglo-Irish, he saw an opportunity to save two of the Three Kingdoms for the King. So, leaving the Queen in France, he set sail for Ireland and, towards the end of September 1648, reached Kilkenny. There he formally dissolved the Confederacy and declared Rinnuccini a rebel, forcing him to leave the country. The Parliamentary forces were quick to respond. Monck and Coote secured Carrickfergus and Londonderry from Monro and Stewart respectively, thus keeping the Ulster Scots in check. In Scotland, too, the Covenanters of Galloway and Ayrshire marched on Edinburgh with 6,000 men to demand that there should be no more negotiating with the King. These protesters were known as Whigs, and gave their name to the great political party. Events reached their climax in 1649, when Charles was tried and executed in London.

News of the beheading of Charles was received with revulsion by Covenanters of all shades of opinion in both Scotland and Ulster. The Belfast Presbytery drew up a 'Representation' in February condemning "the Sectarian Party" of the English Parliament as "proceeding without rule of example to the trial of the King and as putting him to death with cruel hands". It must be said, however, that, in stirring up a Second Civil War, Charles had probably forfeited his right to live. Following the King's death, Ormond immediately proclaimed Charles II King at Cork and continued the War in the name of the new King in April 1649. Enniskillen then declared for the King. Monro escaped his English captors and led his beloved Scots again. Joining with Clanricarde he took Sligo. At this point O'Neill and Monck agreed to a local truce, but were defeated by Inchiquin at Dundalk. Unfortunately for the Royalists, however, the Parliamentary forces in Dublin were reinforced now by 2,000 Ironside veterans, and on 2 August 1649 Jones defeated Ormond's army at Rathmines, just south of that city. A fortnight later Oliver Cromwell arrived in Dublin to settle his accounts and to restore this "Bleeding Nation of Ireland to its former happiness and tranquillity". His campaign was exactly what he meant it to be – quick and cruel, but effective. The actual events have been much coloured by Restoration propaganda.

Cromwell's campaign against the Royalist forces began with the storming of Drogheda on 11 September 1649. The subsequent massacre involved primarily the English Royalist garrison and there is no foundation for the later fictions of indiscriminate slaughter of the whole civilian population.

The fall of Drogheda was enough, however, to persuade O'Neill that the time had come for an alliance with Ormond, but this made little difference to the Ironsides, now the finest army in Europe. In October they took Wexford and, on finding evidence of atrocities committed against the town's Protestant inhabitants, gave no quarter to the Irish garrison. By the end of November O'Neill had died and the only Ulster strongholds left in Royalist hands were Charlemont and Enniskillen, while the Protestant Royalist garrisons of Cork, Youghal and Kinsale had joined Cromwell of their own volition. When the Lord Lieutenant and General for the Parliament of England left Ireland on 26 May 1650 he was confident that his deputies would be able to finish the war soon, and that the Gaelic aristocracy was doomed, its caste system of social order destroyed for all time. He left in command the fine soldier Henry Ireton.

But now Cromwell had to face the Scottish Lion in the North. The Covenanters were angered by the beheading of the King and the increasing coolness of the Puritan party towards Presbyterianism. Accordingly a deputation had been sent, first to The Hague, and then to Breda, for the purpose of laying before the dissolute young Charles II the conditions on which they would accept him as king. These he accepted, but he was never to forgive the humiliation. In the summer of 1650 he journeyed to Scotland and on 16 August signed the Declaration of Dunfermline acknowledging his own and his parent's sins in opposing the Covenant, and admitting the "exceeding great sinfulness... of that treaty and peace made with the bloody Irish rebels, who treacherously shed the blood of so many of his faithful and loyal subjects in Ireland". This so compromised Ormond that it spelled the end of the precarious union of Royalists in Ireland. For Charles it meant a Covenant Army, well over 1,000 men of whom were Galwegians. They proved no match for Cromwell, who defeated them at Dunbar on 3 September 1650. Ormond sailed for France on 11 December, leaving Clanricarde as his deputy, for he felt his presence was now an embarrassment to his cause. The following year Charles II was defeated at Worcester and also retired into exile in France. The War in Ireland continued for almost two more years. Clanricarde finally surrendered on 28 June 1652 and was allowed to retire to his English estate at Somerhill in Kent. When Irishbofin Island surrendered early in the following year, Rory Moore, last of the Loigse Cruthin, made his way secretly to Ulster, Land of the Cruthin, where he lived out his days in seclusion as a fisherman.

Cromwell's designs for the conquered Ireland were embodied in an Act of Settlement passed by the 'Long Parliament' in England in August 1652. This provided for an extensive forfeiture of land in Ulster, Leinster and Munster, ten counties of which were set aside to repay the 'Adventurers' and to remunerate the Parliamentary soldiers. While the leaders of the rebellion had forfeited all rights to their land and property, all others who had not "manifested their constant good affection to the Commonwealth of England" were to suffer partial forfeiture, losing one fifth, one third or two thirds of their estates, according to the degree of their "delinquency". A scheme was made whereby they would be obliged to accept lands in Connacht and Clare equal in value to the land which remained to them. The Irish prisoners-of-war were allowed to enlist in the service of European nations and about 40,000 did so, chiefly going to Spain. Some two hundred persons were executed for their parts in the massacres of 1641, among them Sir Phelim O'Neill. Roman Catholic priests were outlawed and many impoverished families were transported to the West Indies. The Episcopalians also suffered, as did the Presbyterian people of Antrim and Down, for it was decided that they should be transported south, away from the Scottish mainland and continued support from Ayrshire (Carrick) and Galloway.

Although it was first announced that all 'transplantable' persons should remove themselves by 1 May 1654 and that they should be liable to death if they didn't, permission to delay for individuals was freely given. In April 1653, Cromwell dissolved the Rump Parliament and ruled as Lord Protector, and a change of policy towards the leading Ulster Scots meant that their transportation south was not carried into effect. Neither was the subsequent settlement of Ireland by Cromwellian soldiers a success, for not only did they need the Irish as tenants but, albeit strict attempts to prevent them, they intermarried with the Catholic Irish and within a generation many became Catholics and fought for the Jacobite cause. The only lasting effect of the Cromwellian Settlement as a whole was the complete fusion of the Pre-Normans and Anglo-Irish, and this amalgam was Celtic in language only. In 1654, Cromwell despatched his son, Henry, to be ruler of Ireland and under his firm but mild government, an increase in liberty was granted to Catholic, Presbyterian and Episcopalian alike, and Ireland began to prosper again. During the remaining years of the Protectorate, the ministers of the extreme Covenanting sect gained a tremendous hold over the People of the Cruthin, especially in Galloway and Ayrshire. This was to have a profound influence on following events. Ministers were allowed to return to Ulster and there was now no doubt that the Cruthinic element was predominant in the North. An Irish State paper of 1660 states that "there are 40,000 Irish and 80,000 Scots in Ulster ready to bear arms, and not above 5,000 English in the whole province besides the army".

Following the death of "God's Englishman" Cromwell, "our Chief of Men", there was a year of anarchy, brought to a close by the restoration of Charles II in 1660. Charles's first act was to restore the Episcopalian church in the Three Kingdoms, and in 1661 an Act of Conformity was passed which required every minister who officiated in a parish church to conform to the Episcopal Church and the Prayer Book. 'Nonconformist' ministers were ejected from their churches (in all, 64).

Persecution of the Galloway Presbyterians had to wait for a year, since Charles was aware that in Scotland he would have to progress in stages. In the autumn of 1661, however, the former Presbyterian minister of Crail, James Sharp, accepted the post of Archbishop of St Andrews, Primate of Scotland, and the Parliament of 1662 confirmed the return of prelacy. Throughout most of Scotland the ministers submitted, but not so in Galloway. There the people resisted and this resistance resulted in the economic ruin of Galloway between 1662 and 1666. Government troops under Sir James Turner occupied and terrorised the whole area. Courts of High Commission were re-introduced and hundreds of Covenanters were fined, imprisoned, tortured or deported to the Colonies. Eventually, this could no longer be borne, and on 13 November 1666 the Pentland Rising was initiated at Dalry. On 21 November a Covenanter force of about 1,000 men assembled at the Brig O'Doon, near Ayr and marched on Edinburgh. On 28 November at Rullian Green, at the foot of the Pentland hills, they were routed, and many fled to Ulster and Holland. Following the Rising the persecution of Galloway was increased under Sir William Bannatyne, whose murders, rapes and robberies were so numerous that the government itself became sickened. In 1669 an Act of Indulgence was proffered to the Galwegians, but it was not enough for them and only four ministers in the whole of Galloway subscribed to it.

In Ulster, on the other hand, the Presbyterians had learned to live with the prelacy as they had done before and because of this Charles II was so well disposed towards them that he granted to the Ulster ministers a Regium Donum or Royal Bounty. And so, for the 12 years following 1670, there was really nothing that could be remotely described as persecution against them in Ulster. It was this difference between the two regions which resulted in a final concentration of the People of the Cruthin in Ulster, because of the influx from Galloway of many of her impoverished citizens.

On 13 August 1670 the Scottish government passed the notorious Black Act, which made field preaching an offence punishable by death. To this barbarous legislation the increasingly impoverished hill folk of Galloway uttered a defiance whose fire the government attempted to extinguish in blood. In 1678 the arrival of the Highland Host (Norse-Airgiallans) under James Graham of Claverhouse, 'Bonnie Dundee' to his followers but 'Bluidy Clavers' to his opponents, marked the beginning of a grim final decade of persecution in Galloway. These Highlanders were:

"authorised to take free quarter, to seize all horses for carrying their sick men, ammunition and other provisions, and are indemnified against all pursuits, civil and criminal, for anything they do, whether killing, wounding, apprehending, or imprisoning such as shall make opposition to authority".

When the Highlanders returned to their homes at seed-time, as was the custom of such 'Gaelic' raiding parties, their place was taken by English dragoons under their own officers, who gave orders to shoot on sight. On Sunday 1 June 1679 Claverhouse and his troops attacked a field meeting or conventicler at Drumclog, but were defeated by the Covenanters. On 22 June, however, a badly-led army of Covenanters were defeated at Bothwell Bridge. Following this a merciless persecution of the Galloway Cruthin was initiated. A Test Act was passed in August 1681 which obliged them to accept the complete authority of the King in all matters civil and ecclesiastical, and to renounce Presbyterianism. Courts were set up to enforce this, and these were presided over by Claverhouse's brothers and such monsters as Sir Robert Grierson of Lagg. Innocent, suspected and guilty alike were subjected to extreme torture and then either imprisoned on the Bass Rock, or in Blackness Castle. Many others were transported to the colonies to be sold as slaves. Of these events Claverhouse himself wrote:

> "In the meantime we quartered on the rebelles, and indevoured to destroy them by eating up their provisions; but they quickly perceived the dessein, and soued their corns on untilled ground. After which we fell in search of the rebelles, played them hotly with pairtys, so that there were severall taken, many fleid the country and all were dung from their hants; and then rifled so their houses, ruined their goods, and imprisoned their servants, that their wyfes and childring were broght to sterving; which forced them to have recourd to the safe conduct, and mid them glaid to renounce their principles".

The Courts continued their violent work until all the Scottish prisons were full and those who escaped hanging were transported into slavery in the West Indies.

In October 1684 James Renwick of Moniaive assumed the leadership of the Covenanters and published his *Apologetical Declaration* against the King and his ministers. The government replied immediately by an Abjuration Oath renouncing the Declaration, which was to be taken in addition to the Test all over the south-west. At the same time the Privy Council passed an Act which stated that:

> "The lords of his majesty's privy council do hereby ordain any person who owns, or will not disown, the late treasonable document (the Apologetical Declaration), whether they have arms or not, to be immediately put to death".

This opened the way for summary execution without trial and the following period, covering the autumn of 1684 and the whole of 1685, became known as the 'Killing Times'. Although by this time a milder persecution had returned to Ulster, that area had continued to prosper for its citizens, especially in Antrim and Down. Galloway itself continued to decline economically and for the following 50 years was easily the most depressed area in Scotland. In fact, not only was trade virtually non-existent, but the harvests were often so bad that a state of famine existed. The people became so poor that the term Galwegian and Creenie, which derives from Cruithnigh (Cruthin) became terms of deprecation, although the latter term continued to be used in Galloway down to the nineteenth century. Creenie may still linger in Ulster as the family name Creeney or Creaney, so common in Armagh and Down. Furthermore the growing prosperity and relative religious tolerance of Ulster attracted not only the remnants of the impoverished Galloway Cruthin, but also Puritans, Quakers and other Dissenters, mainly from the Northern Counties of England and especially from Yorkshire and Durham.

The year 1685 was a year of Destiny, not only for the Children of the Cruthin in Ulster and Galloway, but for the British Peoples as a whole. On 6 February Charles II died as a Roman Catholic and his brother James II, who may well have poisoned him to prevent Charles legitimising his natural son, the Duke of Monmouth, ascended the Throne. At this time the inhabitants of the growing town of Belfast (pop 2,000) sent a congratulatory address to the new King. But James was an avowed Roman Catholic, and his three year reign and its immediate aftermath constituted the greatest threat yet to the Returned Cruthin. The fears of the whole protestant population of Ireland were first engendered by the recall of Ormond, whose Protestant sympathies were not in accord with James's design for Ireland. According to Lord Macauley, James also "obtained from the obsequious Estates of Scotland, as the surest pledge of their loyalty, the most sanguinary law that has ever in our island been enacted against Protestant Nonconformists". With this law and the dragoons of Claverhouse he wasted and oppressed Galloway still more, the atrocities culminating with the foul murder of the Wigton Martyrs, Margaret Maclachlan and Margaret Wilson in May.

But in England James was forced to tread warily. The Duke of Monmouth was alive and well, an exile in Holland, and a claimant for the throne. Along with Monmouth's supporters were the refugee Scots under the Earl of Argyle, Mac Callum More, Chief of the Clan Campbell. Mac Callum More returned to Scotland in June and tried to raise his clan for the Presbyterian cause, but was captured and executed. A merciless vengeance was then wrought by his conquerors on the people of Argyle. Athol hanged as many Campbells as he could, and the country around Inverary was laid waste to an extent of 30 miles. Meanwhile Monmouth had landed in the West Country of England but, after a short campaign, was defeated at the Battle of Sedgemoor on 6 July, and executed on 15 July. Following this the Bloody Assize opened by Judge Jeffreys against Monmouth's followers made James's name hated throughout the West Country.

Although thus triumphant, James's Catholic design was ironically thwarted by anti-Protestant legislation enforced by his cousin, Louis XIV of France. The Revocation of the Edict of Nantes suppressed all the privileges granted by Henry IV and Louis XIII to the Huguenots, inhibited the exercise of the Protestant religion, enjoined the banishment of all its Ministers within 15 days, held out rewards for converts, and prohibited keeping schools, or bringing up children, in any but the Roman Catholic religion. Dragoons were sent into Languedoc, Dauphiné and Provence to enforce the decree, and it has been estimated that some half-million Huguenots left France as a result. They migrated mostly to the British Isles, Holland and Germany, and brought with them their arts, industry, and resentment. Most important, perhaps, of those who left France for Holland was the Duke of Schomberg, who was a Marshal of France. At this time the Stadholder of the Dutch Republic was William, Prince of Orange, who was married to James II's elder daughter, his cousin Mary. William's acceptance of Schomberg as the General of his armies was to have important consequences for Ulster. Ulster was also to receive many Huguenots, whose Calvinist form of worship made their assimilation into the Presbyterian community a rapid one. It is interesting to note that those who came from the Protestant Orange district in Southern France owed an allegiance to William's House which can be dated as far back as the eighth century. However, as far as the Catholic Design was concerned, the flood of persecuted Protestants into England made James's task well-nigh impossible.

In Ireland, nevertheless, James felt he could progress as planned. In 1686 he appointed his brother-in-law, Clarendon, Lord Lieutenant of Ireland, and an ardent Roman Catholic, Richard Talbot, both Earl of Tyrconnell and General of the Forces in the island. Tyrconnell proceeded to dismiss all 'Englishmen' out of the army, disband the Protestant regiments and replace them with Roman Catholics. In January 1687 the figurehead Clarendon was dismissed and Tyrconnell became Lord Lieutenant. Although it can be argued that James, by means of Tyrconnell, merely effected a return to rule by majority opinion in Ireland, there was much more to the situation than that. To the Scotch-Irish (Scoto-Hibernici) as they now knew themselves, James was that Duke of York who, as Viceroy of Scotland under Charles II, had "amused himself with hearing Covenanters shriek and seeing them writhe while their knees were beaten flat in the boots" (Lord Macauley). It was well known that Tyrconnell's real intention was to drive all the recent settlers out of Ireland, to destroy the Protestant faith in general, and to restore the old Gaelic hegemony. While many of the Protestants prepared for the inevitable defiance, others emigrated to England, where they further enhanced the fears of its Protestant majority as to James's intentions. Following his abolition of the Test Act, James passed two Declarations of Indulgence, the first in 1687 and a fresh one in 1688 whereby toleration was extended to Dissenter and Catholic alike. But to the English Episcopalian of the time the problem was not primarily religious. He feared the political implications of the English Catholicism more than its theology; he feared the absolute nature of its claim to represent the ultimate in social order more than its specific ceremonies; but most of all he began to fear for his country's parliamentary system of government. For, with all his faults (and what 'race' or people has been without them?) the Englishman had created a form of democracy which has been unequalled in the history of civilisation.

As loyalty to James ebbed in England, so the civil power of Roman Catholics increased in Ireland. By the autumn of 1688 all the judges in Ireland were Catholics, as were almost all the highest officers of the State. On 5 November, however, William of Orange landed in England with his army, and by the end of the year the King had abdicated and fled to France. Meanwhile the regiment of Lord Mountjoy, which was one of the few essentially Protestant ones left, was ordered to leave Londonderry, which was to be garrisoned by the Catholic MacDonnells under Lord Antrim. Fearing a repetition of the events of 1641, 13 Apprentice Boys of Derry shut its gates against the government troops, and initiated a series of events which will be remembered by all people who hold courage in high honour. Enniskillen followed suit, and throughout Ulster defence associations were set up and councils of war elected. On 13 February William and Mary were proclaimed King and Queen of England. On

12 March 1689 James II landed at Kinsale from France and marched north to destroy the last affront to his authority. On 18 April he commenced the Siege of Londonderry, which lasted a total of 105 days, the longest in British history. During that time one third of the City's 30,000 inhabitants died of injuries, famine and disease. At last, on 28 July, Derry was relieved by the *Mountjoy* and two other vessels. On the day the siege was raised, 31 July, the brave Enniskilleners added to their glory the defeat of James's troops under Macarthy at Newtownbutler. News also reached James that the Scottish Highlanders (Jacobites) had been defeated at the Pass of Killiecrankie four days earlier. A fortnight later Schomberg landed at Groomsport, County Down, and then marched north to capture Carrickfergus.

Finally on 14 June 1690, King William himself landed at Carrickfergus and bonfires were lit on all the hills of Antrim and Down (Old Ulidia/ Old Ulster). At Loughbrickland in County Down the Protestant King reviewed an army composed of Protestants from all over Europe. About half of the 36,000 men were English and the other regiments were from Scotland, Finland, Brandenburg, Holland and Switzerland. Last but not least stood the Huguenots from France with the people of Derry, Enniskillen and the rest of Ulster. All were Protestants except that magnificent unit, the Dutch Blue Guards, who were Catholics. All fought for the love of William, Prince of Orange, King of the Three Kingdoms, at the immortal Battle of the Boyne on 1 July (11 July in modern calendars and celebrated on Bonfire Night) when they decisively defeated James's Irish and French troops. The victory was spoiled by the death of both Schomberg and Walker of Derry in the battle. James fled hotfoot back to France, leaving his Irish general Patrick Sarsfield to defend Limerick, which he did with brilliance.

William returned to England, but his army under Ginkel captured Athlone on 1 July 1691 and defeated St Ruth and the Irish Catholic forces at Aughrim on 12 July. Waiting in the wings with his own army was a remarkable character named Balldearg O'Donnell. He had arrived from Spain shortly after the Battle of the Boyne claiming to be a lineal descendant of the ancient 'Gaelic' Kings of Tyrconnell in Ulster. He also claimed to be the O'Donnell 'with a red mark' (ball dearg) who, according to ancient prophecy, was destined to lead his followers to victory. Many ordinary Ulster Roman Catholics had flocked to his standard, causing great hostility on the part of Tyrconnell who saw him as a threat to his own earldom. Balldearg thus remained aloof from the Battle of Aughrim. He proceeded to join the standard of William with 1200 men on 9 September 1691, and marched to assist in the reduction of the Jacobite town of Sligo. This garrison surrendered on 16 September 1691, on condition that they were conveyed to Limerick. Balldearg remained loyal to William and later entered his service in Flanders, with those of his men who elected to follow him. On 3 October 1691, the war finally ended with the surrender of Limerick after a heroic defence, and the 'Glorious Revolution' was complete.

The opening of new opportunities for trade, and the cheapness of land laid waste in Ulster, allowed one last wave of immigration from Scotland during the final ten years of the seventeenth century. It was estimated by Archbishop Synge 20 years later that about 50,000 Scots settled in Ulster during this decade. From this time on, Ulster was recognised as British and Protestant and so it has remained to this day. The settlement of the Huguenot Louis Crommelin in Lisburn helped in an already established Linen industry, which was to set the pattern for its industrial prosperity. The 'British' concept was further enhanced in the mainland by the Union of Scotland and England in 1707, a union bitterly resented by many Scottish Highlanders, particularly the Jacobites after the notorious Massacre of Glencoe.

But the People of the Cruthin, the Scotch Irish, were to make the greatest of all their migrations in the eighteenth century and that was to be a New World. Pressurised by Southern Gaelic expansion into Scotland earlier in the Christian era, they had at last returned to the lands of their ancient British ancestors. In every sense of the words they had remained loyal and true. They had maintained the authority of Charles I, had refuted that of Cromwell's Parliamentarians, and had protested against the execution of the King. They had defended Derry and Enniskillen with immortal honour and glory. They had saved Ireland for the British crown and if Ireland had fallen, so too would Scotland and perhaps even England as well. But all this passed for nothing. For the English Church was Episcopalian and the ascendancy which now established itself in Ireland was thus an Episcopalian Anglo-Irish one, ie the 'English in Ireland'.

Having reduced the rebellious Roman Catholics by the harsh Penal Laws under William, the High-Church Party had gained in strength and by the reign of Queen Anne (1702–1714) were pressing for complete conformity. In 1703 a Test Act was passed which required all office holders in Ireland to take the sacrament of the Anglican Church. Although ostensibly passed to further discourage Catholicism, the real object of the Act was to place the Presbyterians on the same plane of impotence. Presbyterian ministers had now no official standing and marriages performed by them were null and void. To the High Churchmen they were actually inferior to Catholic priests, who were considered lawfully ordained in the line of apostolic succession. Presbyterians and other Dissenters could not now serve in the army, the militia, the civil service, the municipal corporations, the teaching profession or the commission of the peace. At Belfast the entire Corporation was expelled, and Londonderry lost 10 of its 12 aldermen.

Yet, for all that, the Presbyterians had long made their adjustments to religious restrictions, and most bishops of the Church of Ireland were especially tolerant in an age of bigotry. Indeed, Archbishop William King was prominent in his expression of abhorrence to the Archbishop of Canterbury, not only of the risks of increasing alienation of the Presbyterians, but of English commercial avarice in restricting the Irish woollen trade and the practice of rack-renting by landlords, whereby a farmer's land would be sold to the highest bidder when his lease ran out. The most unkind cut was the selling of land in Ulster, which had been drained and cultivated by the thrifty Scotch-Irish, to two or more Catholic families who could only continue to live there at mere subsistence level. The final straw came with the drought of the 'teen years of the eighteenth century. This ruined crops, including flax, so that farmers, weavers and townspeople suffered alike. In 1716, sheep were afflicted with the 'rot' and many died. In general, there were severe frosts and prices soared. Thus, in 1717, began the Great Migration of the Cruthinic peoples to America.

The first wave of migration to Pennsylvania (1717–1718) was enough to arouse the English conscience and in 1719 and Act of Parliament was passed to permit Dissenters to celebrate their own form of worship. But rack-renting continued and from 1725 to 1729 there was such an exodus of Ulster Presbyterians to the south-eastern tier of counties in Pennsylvania that their political influence was quickly becoming considerable. That influence was directed increasingly against England. A 'feed-back' into Ulster itself helped to make it a centre of radicalism, which was embodied in the establishment of the great newspaper the *Belfast News-Letter* in 1737. By 1738 Scotch Irish settlers had pioneered their way from Pennsylvania into Virginia, two modern counties of which, Augusta and Rockbridge, claim to be the most Scotch Irish, and thus Cruthinic, in the present United States. By 1738 their Orange County, with its county seat in the Piedmont, embraced most of the Valley of Virginia, and also much of what is now West Virginia.

The winter of 1739–40 was known in Ulster as 'the time of the black frost', because of the darkness of the ice and the lack of sunshine. This severe weather caused famine all over the island and a further wave of migration from Ulster (1740–41). The new arrivals in America now generally went through Pennsylvania down into the Valley of Virginia. Here the McDowell family especially distinguished themselves and thus did the Cruthin become the men of Shenandoah. Others crossed the first range of the Alleghenies to settle in the valleys of (Present) Highland and Bath counties. From Virginia the line of settlement passed into the Piedmont country of North and South Carolina, and there, as in Virginia and Pennsylvania, German settlements were also effected. A third important group were Highland Scots, including the family of Flora MacDonald herself, driven from their homeland following the defeat of Bonnie Prince Charlie (Charles Edward Stuart) at the Battle of Culloden in 1745, followed later by the brutal 'Highland Clearances' (Scottish Gaelic Fuadach Nan Gàidheal, 'the expulsion of the Gael').

Until the 1750s there had been very little opposition to settlement by the Indians. This was due to the intelligent and peaceful policy of the Pennsylvania Quakers and to the absence of Indian settlement in the Valley of the Shenandoah. News of the success of the Scotch Irish settlements, advertised effectively by the Governors of North Carolina, caused a fresh migration from Ulster during the period 1754–55. From then on, however, the French and Indian War began, and for the next ten years the Scotch Irish frontiersmen were fighting for their lives. Learning quickly from their enemies, they rose to a man against the Indians, and, using similar methods of warfare, carried the war into Indian territory. Their destruction of the Indians also helped to end the French control of the Ohio Valley. In 1759 Wolfe captured Quebec from Montcalm and by 1760 the British controlled the whole of Canada. By the Treaty of Paris in 1763, France ceded to Great

Britain all its American territories east of the Mississippi, which included Canada. This peace was shattered, however, by the Indian Uprising known as Pontiac's Conspiracy.

By this time Ulster's economic situation had improved to such an extent that the vacuum left by the Cruthin was being replaced by Southern Irish and Scottish Highlanders. In 1771, however, when the leases on the large estate of the Marquis of Donegal expired in Antrim, the rents of the small farmers were so increased that many could not pay them and were subsequently evicted. Resentment resulted in the formation of secret societies such as the Protestant Hearts of Steel, and a final wave of emigration to America from 1771 to 1775. By the end of 1775 at least a quarter of a million Ulstermen had left the Land of the Cruthin during a 58 year period. To America (Columbia to the British) they brought a hatred of Aristocratic Landlordism. They were the first to declare for Independence in 1776 and they composed the flower and backbone of Washington's Army in the Revolutionary War which followed. Their cause was advocated by the *Belfast News-Letter*, and the contemporary Harcourt wrote that "The Presbyterians in the North are in their hearts Americans". Following the War, emigration slowed and it was as Americans, rather than Scotch Irish, that the Cruthin joined the advance across the Alleghenies in the fight for the West. There are many modern Americans, however, who still trace their descent from the Ancient Kindred. Not all of these are Presbyterians, for many became Methodist and Baptists according to conscience.

The American Revolution was to have a profound effect on the further history of Ireland in general, and of Ulster in particular. When France and Spain joined the Americans in 1778, an invasion of Ireland was feared and an armed militia was formed. These Volunteers were Protestants, and they quickly became a political force in the fight for Irish parliamentary independence. But it was in Belfast that those heights of radical political philosophy were reached which gave the own the name of the 'Athens of the North'. In 1780 the Belfast Volunteers issued an address to Henry Grattan and Barry Yelverton on the theme of the independent rights of Ireland. In 1784 the inhabitants of the town pressed for Parliamentary Reform and the Emancipation of Roman Catholics. In 1789 they welcomed the French Revolution, while in 1791 they celebrated the second anniversary of the storming of the Bastille and read avidly Thomas Paine's *Rights of Man*, written in answer to Burke's *Reflections on the Revolution in France*. The natural extension of these sentiments was the invitation of the young Dublin lawyer Theobald Wolfe Tone to Belfast on 14 October 1791 and the foundation there of the Society of United Irishmen "to form a brotherhood of affection among Irishmen of every religious persuasion". The following year the Society formed a newspaper, the *Northern Star*, in Belfast and this was edited by Samuel Neilson, the son of the Presbyterian minister of Ballyroney, County Down. The British Prime Minister Pitt was not completely immune to its pressures, and in 1792 and 1793 Relief Acts were passed which gave Catholics the right to vote but not the right to become Members of Parliament.

In 1793, Britain declared War on France, and Pitt pressurised the Irish government to raise a very largely Catholic militia to defend Ireland for the Crown. The Volunteers were at the same time disbanded by Proclamation, and the proprietors of the *Northern Star* prosecuted. The Society of United Irishmen rapidly became a secret, subversive movement dedicated to the overthrow of the state. In 1794 a Church of Ireland clergyman, the Rev William Jackson, landed in Ireland as an agent of the French government, and was captured the following year in possession of a paper which sketched a republican uprising. The paper described the Presbyterian people of Ulster as "the most enlightened body of the nation". Jackson was charged with treason and executed in April 1795. Suspicion also fell on Wolfe Tone, who was thus forced to leave for America. Before he did so, he and the Northern leaders, Tom Neilson, Henry Joy McCracken and Thomas Russell, ascended the Cave Hill outside Belfast, where they swore to overthrow the power of England in Ireland forever.

But the American War of Independence had also closed the door to further emigration from Ulster for the present, and sectarian rivalry for land began to come into prominence again. In September 1795 Catholic 'Defenders' attacked Protestant 'Peep o' Day Boys' at the Diamond in County Armagh, and were defeated in a pitched battle. Out of this skirmish was born the Orange Society, which was to develop later into the Orange Order. In the autumn of 1796 a new force named the yeomanry was enlisted for the government in Ulster, and these were chiefly Orangemen. Yet the majority of the Presbyterian people of Ulster remained true to the ideals of the United Irishmen, who had now received a new convert in the tragic young Protestant aristocrat, Lord Edward Fitzgerald. In March 1797 the government decided to disarm the North, and this was done with cruelty by General Lake. Belfast, in particular, suffered the scourge of the Catholic Monaghan militia. By May the whole island was put under martial law, and many atrocities were committed both by British Army regiments such as the Ancient Britons, a Welsh cavalry regiment, and the Orange yeomen. It is doubtful, however, if United Irish feeling would have remained strong in Ulster if it had not been for the hanging of one of the Presbyterian leaders, William Orr, in September 1797. 'Remember Orr' was a slogan as long imprinted on the Hearts of Antrim as was 'Betsy Gray' later on the Hearts of Down.

The year of 1798 was to be the First Year of Liberty for the United Irishmen. They now had some half-a-million members, of whom about one half were armed, and of these 100,000 were Ulstermen and two-thirds of these were Presbyterians. The rebellion of '98, however, was doomed from the onset. The Northerners realised that they could accomplish little without foreign aid, and this was too slow in coming from the French and their Dutch allies. The almost 'American' Presbyterians were increasingly distrustful of France when she quarrelled with the United States early that year. Furthermore, the arrest of most of the Leinster leaders of the United Irishmen in March 1798, followed two months later by their successors, robbed the Rebellion of truly United Irish leadership. In particular the arrest of Lord Edward Fitzgerald and the Sheares brothers placed the Leinster forces under Catholic, and often priestly, control.

When hostilities actually broke out on 24 May, it quickly took the character of a religious and bloody war in the South. Only in Ulster, among the Presbyterian people of Antrim, Down and East Londonderry, was the Rebellion a truly United Irish one. Even there the Presbyterians were dismayed by the lukewarm support from the Catholics, and finally horrified by the stories of atrocity and massacre of Protestants at Scullabogue on 5 June. On 7 June, however, the United Army of Ulster took Larne and Antrim, but was soon defeated and Henry Joy McCracken captured. On 9 June the Hearts of Down won the Saintfield Skirmish and proceeded to Ballynahinch, where on 13 June they were decisively defeated and their leader Henry Monro captured and hanged. His execution was followed by that of the noble Henry Joy McCracken at Belfast on 17 June. Thus did the rebellion in Ulster collapse.

In Wexford there had been more success, but its sectarian nature had little to do with United Irish ideals. The seal of ignominy was set on the southern movement when 100 Protestant captives were slaughtered indiscriminately at Wexford on 20 June. Paradoxically it was among the loyalist ranks that sectarian animosities were overcome. The Catholics of the militia and yeomanry fought side by side with Orangemen and the force which had contained the rebellion in June was an overwhelming Catholic one. By the time the French arrived at Killala Bay, County Mayo in August and at Lough Swilly in September, the Rebellion was virtually over. Both these expeditions were defeated and Tone, who was with the latter one, was captured. Rather than be hanged, the brave idealist committed an honourable suicide.

As for the Children of the Cruthin, disgusted, dismayed and finally fearful of the new sectarian aspect of 'Irish freedom', many joined the Orange Order, and with some reservation supported the Union of Great Britain and Ireland in 1801. This Union they have fought to maintain ever since. In 1802, one of the '98 leaders, Thomas Addis Emmett, met the First Consul of the French Republic, Napoleon Bonaparte, who promised him aid. Article One of Emmett's revolutionary proclamation provided for the confiscation of all church property, an ideal not entirely relished by the Irish Roman Catholic hierarchy. Emmett's brother Robert planned a new rebellion in 1803, but this was poorly organised and ended in a debacle. Among those who turned out with the Dublin Lawyers' Yeomanry Corps to hunt down the rebels was a young man named Daniel O'Connell.

The loyalty of Irish Roman Catholics with their Protestant fellow-countrymen to the British concept is fully attested by the Napoleonic Wars which followed. New regiments, such as the Connaught Rangers, fought like heroes alongside the famous Inniskillings (the Enniskillen Regiment), and it was such men whom Wellington (himself an Irish Protestant) had in mind when he said "It is mainly due to the Irish Catholics that we all owe our proud pre-eminence in the military career". Indeed it has been estimated that at least half the 'English Army' under Wellington at Waterloo in 1815 were Irishmen. Certainly, according to Wellington himself, "the 27th of Foot (Inniskillings) saved the centre of my line at Waterloo". In 1823 Daniel O'Connell formed the Catholic Association, and within six years Catholic Emancipation was achieved. The organisation of a national police force, the Royal Irish Constabulary, under an enlightened administration in the 1830s took power away from the Orange Order. Following an attack on the Order by the great radical John Hume in 1836, the Grand Lodge formally dissolved itself and its influence declined. In April 1840 O'Connell formed the National Repeal Association backed by the reactionary Archbishop of Tuam. Early support for this also came from the mainly Protestant 'Young Ireland' movement, whose ideals were those of '98. Disillusion with conservative Catholicism came for the Young Irelanders when McHale of Tuam and the bishops insisted that Roman Catholic students at the newly founded Queen's Colleges could not attend lectures in history, logic, anatomy, geology, metaphysics or moral philosophy "without exposing their faith and morals to imminent danger", unless the lecturers were Roman Catholics.

At the same time, only in Ulster were the needs of a soaring population met by industrial expansion. The failure of the staple Potato Crop, and the resultant Great Famine of 1845–49, changed the whole political, economic and social history of the island. Massive emigration to America was forced on a starving and disease-ridden population. Many of these emigrants formed in the USA an unwanted nation within a nation, the Irish-Americans, whose influence on the further history of Ireland was profound, and not always healthy. Following the American Civil War (1861–65), the Irish-Americans formed a recruiting source for the violent anti-British Fenian movement. As Irish nationalism became more and more anti-British, the more unacceptable did any attempt to have Home Rule appear to the loyalists, particularly in Ulster. The 1870s and 1880s, however, became known as the Age of Charles Stewart Parnell, who linked the cause of land reform with that of Home Rule, and moulded the Irish Parliamentary Party into a powerful force. Because of the large Irish Catholic population who had settled in England as a result of the Famine, it was now easier for the Fenian Brotherhood (Irish Republican Brotherhood) to gain influence there. In Northern eyes Parnell's association with the Fenians had sinister implications, and this led to a revival of the Orange Order, which became a truly popular movement in Ulster, combining Episcopalians and Presbyterians, conservatives and liberals, landlords and tenants, employers and workers, in a fierce opposition to Home Rule. More and more to the Ulster people did Home Rule mean Rome Rule.

But the real enemy of British Ireland was not the Roman Catholic Church, which actually excommunicated Fenians, but the rise of a Gaelic nationalism and its identification with Irish nationalism. The greatest poet of Ireland in the nineteenth century was Sir Samuel Ferguson, who was born in Belfast in 1810, of Cruthinic stock. Ferguson typified the Ulster intellectual of his day, intensely proud of his 'Gaelic' heritage, but without the rancour of the xenophobe. In 1872 he published his masterpiece *Congal*, which told of the death of that great Prince of the Cruthin and following his death came the *Lays of the Red Branch*. In 1884, however, was formed the Gaelic Athletic Association, which promoted hurling and Gaelic football, and forbade the playing of 'foreign games'. In 1893 the Anglican Douglas Hyde founded the Gaelic League, which had as its aim the 'de-anglicisation' of Ireland. From this sprang Gaelic Nationalism: "Ireland not free only, but Gaelic as well; not Gaelic only, but free as well". Strangely enough, through the sentimentalists Yeats and Lady Gregory, a pseudo-Celtic Twilight Culture was created, which not only bowdlerised, but Anglicised, the old Gaelic literature out of all recognition. The political manifestation of the 'Gaelic Revival' was the foundation of 'Sinn Fein' (We Ourselves) in 1905. This movement soon attracted and was taken over by the veteran Fenians. At the same time there was a growth of Marxist philosophy, and an active socialist movement was led by James Connolly and Jim Larkin. Confronted by such threats, coupled with the loss of the *Titanic* on 15 April 1912, the British known as Ulstermen formed an Ulster Unionist Council to fight Home Rule.

Civil War now seemed inevitable. In 1912 the Ulstermen signed a Covenant whereby they swore to use "all means which may be found necessary to defeat the present conspiracy to set up a Home Rule parliament in Ireland". It was obvious that what they really feared was the form of government which was to follow Home Rule. 1913 saw the formation of the Ulster Volunteer Force under Sir Edward Carson and Sir James Craig, the Irish Citizen's Army under James Connolly and the Irish Volunteers under Eoin MacNeill of the Gaelic League. But the outbreak of the Great War in 1914 averted civil hostilities, and Irishmen of all persuasions sailed to Europe to fight for the King and Empire. The IRB (Irish Republican Brotherhood) leaders saw this as an opportunity for revolt, and a Republican Uprising was effected without success during Easter 1916. This insurrection and the subsequent execution of its leaders evinced "a terrible beauty" in the eyes of Yeats at a time when thousands of Irishmen were dying unsung in Flanders. On 1 July 1916 the 36th (Ulster) Division sustained 5,500 casualties at the battle of the Somme, a sacrifice greater by far, as were the losses of the mainly Catholic 16th (Irish) Division at Guillemont, Ginchy and Messines. Nevertheless in 1918 Sinn Fein won a majority of Irish seats at Westminster, and the first self-styled Dail Eireann (Government of Ireland) met in Dublin the following year. There followed a bloody War of Independence fought between the British Irish and the Irish Republican Army, the British Irish being aided by the 'Black and Tans', who merely alienated the population.

The British Prime Minister, David Lloyd George, tried a compromise settlement in 1920, which provided for separate parliaments in Northern and Southern Ireland. Northern Ireland consisted of the whole of Old Ulster (Old Ulidia), ie Antrim and Down, as well as four other counties of the English Provincial configuration of contemporary Ulster, which consisted of nine counties. The other 26 counties became the Irish Free State in 1922 following an Anglo-Irish Treaty, but the Dominion Status of the new State was not acceptable to the Republicans. Civil War then erupted between Pro- and Anti-Treaty factions, the former led by Michael Collins, the latter by Eamon de Valera. During the last six months of this War, nearly twice as many republican prisoners were executed by the Authorities of the Free State as were executed by the British in the period from 1916 to 1921. It all ended with a Government victory in 1923.

In 1926 de Valera formed his Fianna Fail (Warriors of Destiny) Party. The Free State Party (Cumann na nGaedheal) lost power to Fianna Fail in 1923 and changed its name to Fine Gael (Tribe of Gaels) the following year. How many of either party were Gaels in either language culture or ethnic origins is open to discussion. In 1937 de Valera produced a new Constitution, which was a documentation of contemporary Roman Catholic social theory. Not unnaturally it had its attractions for the Catholics of Northern Ireland, since Craigavon had stated on 24 April 1934, in response to de Valera's Catholic State, that "we are a Protestant parliament and a Protestant State". Yet from the outset Carson had pleaded that the Catholic minority should have nothing to fear from the Protestant majority: "Let us take care to win all that is best among those who have been opposed to us in the past. While maintaining intact our own religion, let us give the same rights to the religion of our neighbours". That that reconciliation was not achieved was due to faults on both sides.

The German Intelligence Services (Abwehr) were very effective in Northern Ireland at this time. Their top spy in Ireland just before the Second Great War was the archaeologist Adolf Mahr, whom de Valera installed as Director of the National Museum in Dublin. Born in Austria, he was a 'serious scholar' and in Dublin became a powerful force. His appointment as Museum Director when there were excellent applicants for the post from Britain, seemed to illustrate the strength of the hatred of all things British prevailing in Éire in the years following Partition. In fact it was another German who was first appointed, Mahr succeeding him on his early death. Like many other scholarly Germans, Mahr was a dedicated Nazi, and his agents in the German Academic Exchange, such as Herr Jupp Hoven, had much to do with the Belfast Blitz of 15 April and 4 May 1941, when over 1,000 people lost their lives.

During the War (1939–45) the Irish Free State remained neutral. The Gaelic Nationalists had much in common with Fascist Spain but baulked at assisting the German Nazis. Both Britain and the USA considered the seizure of Southern Irish bases, but Northern Ireland kept the Atlantic lifeline open. Winston Churchill summed it all up when he said:

"But for the loyalty of Northern Ireland and its devotion to what has become the cause of 30 Governments or Nations, we should have been confronted with slavery or death and the light which now shines so strongly throughout the world would have been quenched".

We should remember with gratitude too, however, those excellent Southern Irishmen who went North and East to join the British Army and fought with such valour for the Freedom of the World.

Following the War, a Republic of Ireland was formally inaugurated in Southern Ireland on Easter Monday 1949. Emigration to England continued on a large scale, so that a substantial proportion of its inhabitants are today of Irish descent. Gaelic nationalist policy became more and more identified with the Roman Catholic Hierarchy and the Establishment it created was a religio-political one. Gaelic studies soon showed that the Gaels were not the ancient inhabitants of Ireland, and Eoin MacNeill and TF O'Rahilly were aware of this as early as 1937. Subsequently the results of Early Irish Studies, as well as later propaganda, were kept within strict political limits. Most scholarly work did not appear beyond the pages of learned books and journals. And for 80 years after the formation of the Gaelic League, there did not exist a complete textbook of Early Irish History, while most historical works were purely insular in character. But if the culmination of that history is the return of the island to the oldest inhabitants by name, then those people are the People of the Cruthin, the Ancient British, for they are the Ancient Kindred of Ireland.

EPILOGUE

So we have come full circle. It is apparent that there are many nonsense terms in the literature, such as 'Celtic Race', 'Gaelic Race' and 'Irish Race', and these we would deprecate. At the same time, we have retained the distinction between Indo-European stock (the originators of Celtic, German, Greek, Latin, Sanskrit, etc) and non-Indo-European stock (Mesolithic, Neolithic, Atlanto-Mediterranean, etc) merely to give meaning to the word 'Cruthin' as we see it. Given the likely population growth which followed the introduction of an agricultural economy in the Neolithic period, and allowing for genocide, famine and disease, all subsequent immigrations to Ireland were most likely to have been carried out by populations numerically far inferior to those aboriginal peoples who came to be known as Cruthin.

Distribution maps of Blood Groups in the British Isles show that in Ireland, Scotland and the Isle of Man Group O is more common than Group A, while in all the other 'Celtic' areas Group A is more common than Group O. This would seem to confirm that the northerly and westerly parts of the British Isles, were, in general, less affected by the Indo-European invasions of Celts, Germans and Scandinavians. Also of interest in this respect are the ethnic differences in the incidence of the two major congenital neurological malformations anencephalus and spina bifida, in which an important genetic factor is thought to be present. Distribution maps of the British Isles show an increase in incidence from the South and East to the North and West which parallels Blood Group O.[1] Epidemiological studies of children born to residents of Belfast during the years 1964–1968 demonstrated a combined incidence in Belfast of the two defects of 8.7 per thousand (live and still) births (4.2 anencephalus and 4.5 spina bifida), which is the highest recorded in any community to date.[2] Since the inhabitants of Belfast have been shown to be essentially non-Indo-European stock, this high incidence would also seem to confirm our thesis that they are, indeed, the People of the Cruthin.

Originating in the nineteenth century Celtic Romantic Movement, the Celtic myth, however, continues to be pursued by writers of popular history and Irish Nationalist political propaganda. The cell structure of academic elitism protects those 'Celtic Scholars' and 'Professional Archaeologists' who continue to disseminate notions of a Gaelic Aryan Race to which Ireland rightfully belongs. The extension of similar notions of Nordic Man into tools of oppression in Nazi Germany should be an object lesson to those responsible for the education of young persons. As recently as the 5 May 1984, the Irish Association of Professional Archaeologists held a seminar on the "problem of the earliest appearance of Irish-speaking Celts in Ireland". The participants included not only archaeologists but also representatives from linguistic and environmental studies. The question put to the seminar was "when did the Irish first arrive in Ireland?" An 'Irishman' was significantly defined as one who spoke either the earliest attested form of the 'Irish language', ie Gaelic, or a language immediately ancestral to it. Thus the earlier native populations of Ireland were denied the epithet 'Irish' in favour of the Gaels and were designated as mere 'Irelanders'. This indicates the persistence of Gaelic patriotic racialism among an important section of the academic élite, whose political influence among educationalists and the media has been, and continues to be, profound.

The search for the 'Ancient Gael' is, of course, a tale in itself, and has been omitted from the body of the text for the sake of clarity. During the late nineteenth century the 'Ancient Gael' was stated by 'Celtic Scholars' to have inhabited both Britain and Ireland in the Pre-historical period. This theory was finally abandoned, since the 'Proto-Picts' were discovered to have spoken a non-Indo-European language and Scottish Gaelic was seen to be a derivative of archaic Irish Gaelic. The next stage therefore was to place the 'Ancient Gael' firmly in Pre-historic Ireland. Since, however, the Cruthin were the oldest people known in Ireland, and they were cognate with the Picts, the 'Ancient Gael' had to be content with being a superlative Aryan warrior aristocracy. There were now two alternatives: either to describe the Cruthin as 'Celts' or to accept them as 'Pre-Celtic' and then ignore them. This constitutes a form of cultural imperialism akin to that of the 'Anglo-Irish' Ascendancy.

During the late 1960s and early 1970s a number of linguists and archaeologists claimed that a first 'Beaker Movement' of 2,300 BC were

'Q-Celtic' and carried that language to Ireland, while a second 'Beaker Movement' of 2,000 BC were 'P-Celts' and thus carried their language to Britain only. The relative distribution of Blood Groups O and A were cited as indicating the presence of Q-Celts and P-Celts respectively. Such opinions, with neither serious linguistic nor archaeological evidence to support them, were even promoted by the British Broadcasting Corporation.[3] "Received Opinion" now admits that there is "a certain degree of consensus that archaeologists and linguists are justified in confining their search for the first Irishman (sic) to circa the first millennium BC rather than the beginnings of the Early Bronze Age".[4] However the absence of intrusive burial remains in the Late Bronze Age (Dowris) or an intrusive Hallstatt C or La Tène cemetery has led serious archaeologists to resist Gaelic Nationalist pressure and confirm that there is no present evidence for significant intrusion into Ireland from the Neolithic until the early Roman period (c 100 AD). In Britain a major intrusion seems to have been associated with the so-called 'Arras Culture' which appeared in East Yorkshire when the Continental Iron Age was in its 'La Tène I' phase.[5] Hence may have arrived the Parisii and Brigantes in Britain, whence the latter with the Uluti came to Ireland.

Much has been written about the antiquity of early Irish vernacular tradition. Yet oral tradition as preserved in Irish Gaelic is oblivious of the best dated Iron Age structure in the British Isles – the Great Post of Emania, which was ceremonially burned in the first century BC. It was also oblivious of the most strategically important archaeological sites within the small geographical area of the island of Ireland. Most notable of these in the North is the structure known only as the 'Black Pig's Dyke' or 'Worm's Cast'. Extensive remains of this earthen defensive fortification still exist and have been dated by dendrochronology to c 100 BC. Like the unique monument known as the 'Dorsey' at Drummill Bridge in South Armagh the major defensive line, a high bank straddled by two deep ditches, is found on that part of the enclosure facing to the south. These defences of ancient Ulster, and the later Dane's Cast, are not really recognised elsewhere in Ireland and are specifically associated with the early people of Ulster. Furthermore, although Emain Macha was long remembered as political centre of the North, not all the old roads led there. Several also led to another capital, Clogher, which may have been just as important.

The Gaels themselves are, of course, a very important part of Irish and British history, well worthy of the most intensive scientific study. They do not, however, originally belong to Ireland and Ireland does not belong to them. While admiring the early mythology, social structure and legal system of the Gaels, it does not follow that these pertained within the geographical context of Ireland from time immemorial. Classical references to the Pretani had occurred by c 325 BC and if Pictish customs are the remnants of those of the Pretani whom Diodorus mentioned in the first century BC, then Celtic Law was certainly not prevalent in Ireland in the late millenia BC. Neither does it follow that the Gaelic-speaking invaders were of 'pure' 'Celtic' stock. If, as tradition asserts, they originated from the Iberian Peninsula, they must have had other population groups among them at this most westerly limit of the 'Celtic Realms'. It is quite feasible that the Scythian influence apparent in Gaelic Art had its origins in Spain and that tribal names such as Sciathraige, and Scotraige itself, may be Scythian derivatives. Certainly we are assured by Seneca that the Scythians reached Spain and their ability to lose their nationality throughout Europe is well known. Clearly the word Scythia was respected enough by the early Irish Gaelic aristocracy for it to be regarded as the land of ultimate origin of the Sons of Mil. On the other hand, the historian Mela said that the Belgae were Celto-Scythians. Obviously similar traditions were moulded into one in the *Book of the Taking of Ireland*.

The first great leader of the Gaels in Ireland, Tuathal Techtmar, was probably a Roman soldier or auxiliary. Although it was Agricola's frequent theme in retirement,[6] Ireland was never invaded by the Romans themselves. The Gaels seem, however, to have become just as militarily effective. Following their establishment of a power base in Ireland, subsequent contacts with Roman Britain must have taken many forms, including trade, settlement, marriage, gift-giving, slavery, mercenary service and raiding, culminating in their eventual introduction to Christianity. The dynamic of the Gaels and their dependents fed on and contributed to the destabilisation and collapse of Roman Britain. The successful expansion of a slave economy, linked with aggressive militarism, led to the assimilation of the earlier communities, who after a period of bilingualism adopted Gaelic during the fifth and sixth centuries AD. Thus Gaelic became one of the most bizarre branches of Indo-European.[8] Archaeologically these events are evidenced by a clear replacement of earlier Iron Age material by Late Roman types. This was underway by the fourth century AD and by c AD 700 had affected the whole island, appearing latest in Ulster of the Cruthin and Ulaid, which stood late against the Invader Gael.

So it was that the traditions of Ulster were to survive in the earliest Gaelic literature. For example, the story of Iliach from the *Táin bó Cúailgne* reads:

"Iliach was the son of Cas mac Baicc meic Rossa Rúaid meic Rudraige. He was told how the four great provinces of Ireland had been plundering and laying waste the lands of the Ulaid and Cruthin from the Monday at the beginning of Samain until the beginning of spring, and he took counsel with his people 'What better plan could I devise than to go and attack the men of Ireland and win victory over them and avenge the honour of Ulster? It matters not if I myself fall thereafter.'"[9]

The recording of such traditions in the seventh century assumed in Ulster "something of the impetus and cohesiveness of a cultural movement"[10] with the progressive Cruthinic monastery of Bangor as its intellectual centre. Thus Bangor, at the crossroads between Britain and Ireland, was to become the focus of a conservative yet creative activity which was to make Ulster, and thus Ireland, the cradle of modern Western civilisation.

1 July 1986
BELFAST

End Notes

1. Smithells, RW, 'The Epidemiology of Congenital Malformations' in Apley, J, ed, *Modern Trends in Paediatrics*, London, 1970.

2. Elwood, JH and Nevin, NC, 'The Epidemiology of Anencephalus and Spina Bifida in Belfast 1964–68', *Ulster Medical Journal*, Belfast, 1973.

3. Ross, A, 'The Beginning of Europe' in *The Listener*, BBC Publications, 3 January 1974.

4. Mallory, JP, 'The Origins of the Irish' in *The Journal of Irish Archaeology II*, 1984.

5. Salway, P, *Roman Britain*, Oxford, 1981.

6. Dobson, B, 'Agricola's Life and Career' in Kenworthy, J, ed, *Agricola's Campaigns in Scotland*, Edinburgh, 1981.

7. Hamlin, A, *Historic Monuments of Northern Ireland*, Belfast, 1983.

8. Wagner, H, *Studies in the origins of the Celts and of early Celtic civilisation*, Belfast-Tubingen, 1971.

9. O'Rahilly, C, ed, *Táin bó Cúailgne*, Dublin, 1970.

10. Mac Cana, P, 'Mongán mac Fiachna and Immram Brain' in *Ériu*, Vol XXIII, Dublin, 1972.

ADDENDUM

Awonderfully arcane article has appeared recently on the Internet. It is an unpublished paper by the English academic Alex Woolf (University of St Andrews) which he has given several times in different venues. It was originally written in about 2001 as a response to Ewen Campbell's 'Were the Scots Irish?' Antiquity 75 (2001), 285–92.

Woolf says that he had never got around to finally writing it up for publication and although he hoped he would eventually do so he could not see himself getting it done anytime soon. Various academics in the field, such as the Canadian James E Fraser, now in the University of Edinburgh and the Irish-American Thomas Clancy, now in the University of Glasgow, had seen it in draft and responded to it so Woolf felt he should put it into the public domain. He posted it on Academia.edu on 9 April 2012 but it had not been significantly updated since 2005.

Campbell had assumed an obviously Scottish Nationalist approach to propose that Scottish Gaelic Dalriada came first and Irish Dalriada was formed from it and not the other way round. Woolf accepts this on what he feels are linguistic grounds, even though he knows Campbell's archaeological evidence is untenable and his own conclusions are convoluted, but the hypothesis has now established itself in the academic pseudo-historical canon. Frazer downplays the Cruthin in Ireland in his work on the Picts, although it clearly worries him to do so. Clancy is responsible for promoting the notion that St Ninian and St Uinniau (Finnian of Moville) are one and the same person.

Woolf's article contains the usual criticisms of my work and completely misrepresents my view that the Cruthin were the pre-Celtic inhabitants of these Islands, although they later spoke Gaelic ('Irish') and Old British ('Welsh'). This will require an agnotological academic approach to dispel in the future. As he explains in his own words:

"At one time some historians, including the great Eoin MacNeill, believed that the Pretani were the original inhabitants of both Britain and Ireland and that the Gaels had arrived at a late stage in prehistory displacing them from most of Ireland. According to this argument the Cruithni of northern Ireland were the last remnant of the pre-Gaelic inhabitants of the island. It has now become clear that this view is not supported by linguistic, historical or archaeological evidence. If British-speaking Celts ever did settle in Ireland they must have done so subsequently to the development, in situ, of the Gaelic language."

I have further transcribed his words with emphasis on a most remarkable and telling admission, which is self-explanatory:

"Unfortunately the idea that Northern Ireland was British ab origine has proved attractive to certain elements within the Unionist tradition during the political troubles of that province. As a result „Cruithni Studies", to coin a phrase, have become the preserve of Unionist apologists such as Ian Adamson whose most recent book on the Cruithni concludes with a chapter on the Scots-Irish experience in the Appalachians. **Serious historians of early Ireland, tending as they do to have nationalist sympathies or to be politically neutral have tended, understandably, to steer clear of the topic.** Jim Mallory is typical of most serious scholars when he summarises his brief discussion of the topic thus: 'about the only thing the Cruthin hypothesis does emphasise are the continuous interactions between Ulster and Scotland. We might add that whatever their actual origins and ultimate fate, when the Cruthin emerge in our earliest texts they bear Irish names and there is not the slightest hint that they spoke anything other than Irish.'

In typically provocative style Professor Dumville, alluding to this kind of statement in his, so far unpublished, British Academy Rhŷs Lecture in Edinburgh a few years ago (1997?), asked what the evidence for such an assertion might be. I can only imagine that Dumville was questioning whether we had any texts of Cruthnian provenance and whether we could be certain that Gaelic writers, clearly able to

Gaelicise Pictish personal and place names were not doing the same for the Irish Cruithni. Mallory is of course right that there is not the slightest hint that the Cruithni spoke anything other than Irish, just as Dumville is correct, if I understood him, that absence of evidence is not evidence of absence, but is this really all that can be said? St Patrick aside, contemporary literary witness in Ireland begins only in the course of the century between AD 550 and AD 650, and it is true that our sources, the chronicles and hagiography, give us only the name of the Cruithni, which appears periodically between 446 and 774, to suggest their foreignness."

Thus, according to Woolf, it seems acceptable for "serious historians" of early Ireland to have "nationalist" sympathies but not "unionist" ones. The Englishman Richard Warner, formerly of the Ulster Museum, and his colleague the Irish-American JP Mallory, formerly of the Queen's University, Belfast, have spent years following their Quest for the Holy Gael. Their definition of the first 'Irishman' remarkably is someone who spoke the 'Irish' language, ie Gaelic. The bulk of the population before this are relegated to the term 'Irelander'. One would like to say that only an Englishman or an Irish-American could say this with a straight face. But no…Woolf says that "Jim Mallory is typical of most serious scholars". Woolf, by the way, amazingly leaves out the Iveagh Cruthin of Down to the south of Ulster as well as the Cenél Conaill to the west in his article:

"At the beginning of the sixth century the western frontier of the Cruithni seems to have been in the neighbourhood of the Lough Foyle, although by the 570s they had been pushed back beyond the river Bann by the northern Uí Néill. In the East the boundary of the Cruithni seems to have been somewhere in the region of Belfast Lough. Crudely speaking their territory at the dawn of history was equivalent to the modern day counties of Antrim and Londonderry. To the West were the Uí Néill, to the South the Airgialla and to the East the Ulaid. In the middle of this territory, pushed up between the Bush valley and the north coast, lay the lands usually assigned to the Dál Riata in Ireland by modern scholarship. This enclave was entirely surrounded by Cruithni túatha.

Is it not odd that the most Irish people in Britain were, in their Irish territories, surrounded by those Irish people who were described by their countrymen as British? Can it be coincidence? The simplest explanation of this paradox would be to assume that, pace the later synthetic historians and genealogists the Dál Riata and Cruithni were in origin two parts of the same people, perhaps ultimately British in origin, who formed a political, cultural and linguistic bridge between the two islands."

This assertion supports the myth that the Cenél Conaill are "northern Uí Néill", when in reality they are actually Cruthin. And by "British", he means 'from Great Britain', since he seems to deny that epithet to "unionists" and the ancient people of Ireland, mesmerised as he is by the term "Irish".

Actually the people of Scottish Dalriada are Gaelicised native Epidian Pretani and spoke Old British before Gaelic and obviously non-Indo-European before that. They were Gaelicised from Ireland in the Late Roman period by a process of commerce and conquest, as the Venerable Bede has stated. And they now speak Gaelic or Scots with strong Norse elements, and universally, English, though they remain, as they have always been, Epidian Pretani.

The truth is the truth and we are bound by it, as Professor Rene Fréchet of the Sorbonne University in Paris instructed me 30 years ago. Much of what I had written was new to him, and he was amazed and indeed appalled that he had never heard it before. He wanted to translate my work into French. There were those among Irish academia who wished to burn it but their 'politically neutral' counterparts, friends and colleagues in Great Britain did nothing and in doing so supported them.

Adolf Mahr, the German spy-master, tried to return to Ireland after the Second World War but de Valera had had enough of him and would not permit it. However Mahr's influence remained strong in the perpetuation of the Hallstatt myth of early Celtic origins in Austria, the birthplace of both Mahr and that other Adolf, his hero and devoted master. The Gaelic myth itself, which de Valera still promoted, continued to be pursued by Patriot Poets, as well as by writers of popular history and Irish nationalist political propaganda, including "serious historians". The cell structure of academic elitism protected those Celtic scholars who continued to disseminate notions of a Gaelic Aryan Race, to whom Ireland rightfully belonged. The Hallstatt myth is slowly losing ground but is unfortunately now being replaced by the new myths for old: of the Irish/Irelander concoction, as we have seen; of Tartessian 'Celtic' origins; of the primacy of Scottish 'Gaelic' Dalriada; and of the 'Northern Uí Néill'. These myths will create their own difficulties for the citizens of the United Kingdom of Great Britain and Northern Ireland into the foreseeable future. Indeed there may be ramifications for the whole world if the United Kingdom eventually disintegrates and loses its seat on the Security Council of the United Nations. Simply because there are "serious scholars" who remain trapped in Irish, Scottish, Welsh and English nationalist ideologies. We must not allow this to happen.

1 October 2014

APPENDIX 1

CRUTHINIC ART

THE EXACT NATURE OF the sensibility of the Cruthin may be gauged by Pictish influence in Early Christian ornamentation. This is apparent in ornamental stones found on the East Coast of Scotland and England from Shetland to Durham and in parts of Ireland, being strongly characterised by intricate knotwork interlacing. Identical features are also found in the great contemporary illuminated Gospels of Kells, Lindisfarne and Durrow, which together constitute the richest store of the heritage of the British Peoples.

The *Book of Durrow* is a Gospel manuscript named after the Columban foundation of Durrow near Tullamore in Offaly. The manuscript is generally regarded as having been made towards the end of the seventh century AD, perhaps in the 670s. Cruthinic influence is outstanding, probably both through the Cruthinic Magnum Monasterium (Bangor in North Down) and through direct affiliation with Lindisfarne in Northumbria, where Pictish influence was strong. It was kept from at least the eleventh century until the Dissolution, eventually in 1661 coming into the possession of the Cromwellian Henry Jones, who became the Protestant Bishop of Meath and Vice-Chancellor of Trinity College, Dublin.

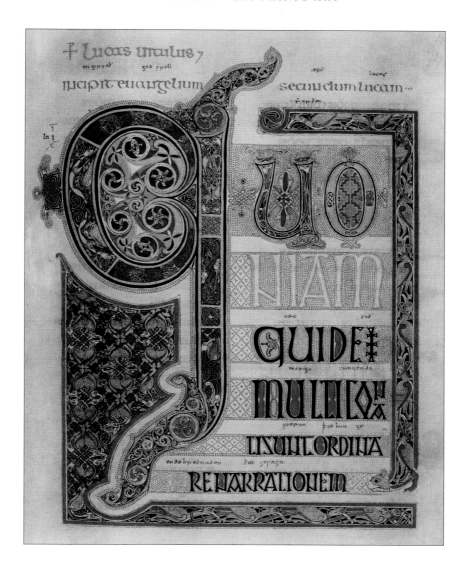

The *Lindisfarne Gospels* were written in honour of Saint Cuthbert by Eadfrith, who was made Bishop of Lindisfarne in AD 698, and were bound by Bishop Ethilward and ornamented by Bilfrith the Achorite. This great work was preserved with the body of the saint at Lindisfarne then carried in flight before the fury of the Vikings and, having rested some years at Durham, finally returned to Lindisfarne Priory, where it stayed until the Dissolution. The finest surviving example of the Pictish Art form, the Gospels are now in the possession of the British Museum.

Universally acknowledged to be the finest achievement in Scottish-Irish manuscript illumination, the *Book of Kells* is now generally assigned to the late eighth or early ninth century when it was written and illuminated by the scribes of Iona. Subsequently it was brought to Kells, where it was known in the eleventh century as 'the great Gospel of Colum Cille' (Columba). Many influences are apparent in its design, notably Coptic and Scythian. The famous Chi-Rho page is also close aesthetically to the beautiful Pictish cross slab from Nigg. By this time, of course, the Cruthin had declined in Ulster.

APPENDIX 2

MAPS

1. Ulster – Land of the Cruthin
2. British Isles genetic markers
3. The British Isles according to Ptolemy
4. Ulster in the seventh century
5. Cráeb Tulcha (Crew Hill)
6. The British Isles in Early Christian Times
7. The British Isles circa AD 1200 indicating the 'Scandinavian' settlements
8. Seventeenth century settlements in Ulster
9. The British Isles circa AD 1700 illustrating the Civil Wars of the Three Kingdoms
10. The United States (Columbia) in AD 1810 indicating the extent of Ulster settlement in the eighteenth century
11. The language of Ulster

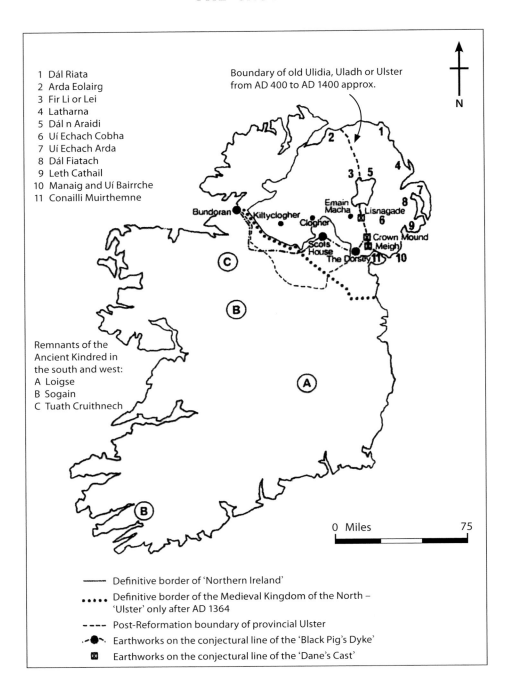

1 Dál Riata
2 Arda Eolairg
3 Fir Li or Lei
4 Latharna
5 Dál n Araidi
6 Uí Echach Cobha
7 Uí Echach Arda
8 Dál Fiatach
9 Leth Cathail
10 Manaig and Uí Bairrche
11 Conailli Muirthemne

Boundary of old Ulidia, Uladh or Ulster
from AD 400 to AD 1400 approx.

N

Remnants of the
Ancient Kindred in
the south and west:
A Loigse
B Sogain
C Tuath Cruithnech

0 Miles   75

———— Definitive border of 'Northern Ireland'

•••• Definitive border of the Medieval Kingdom of the North –
'Ulster' only after AD 1364

- - - - Post-Reformation boundary of provincial Ulster

.-●·. Earthworks on the conjectural line of the 'Black Pig's Dyke'

▨ Earthworks on the conjectural line of the 'Dane's Cast'

1. Ulster – Land of the Cruthin

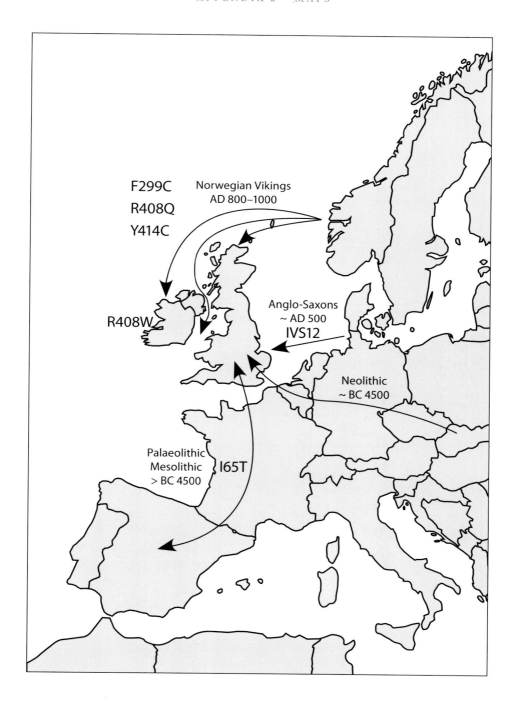

F299C
R408Q
Y414C

Norwegian Vikings
AD 800–1000

R408W

Anglo-Saxons
~ AD 500
IVS12

Neolithic
~ BC 4500

Palaeolithic
Mesolithic
> BC 4500   I65T

2. British Isles genetic markers

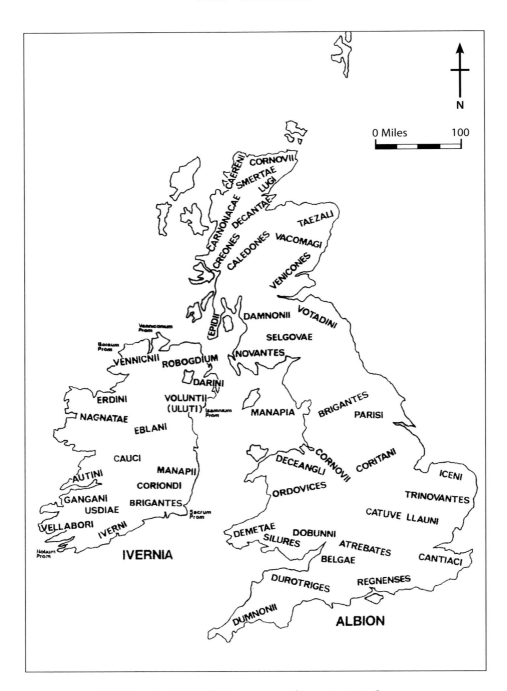

3. The British Isles according to Ptolemy
Sources dated approximately AD 100

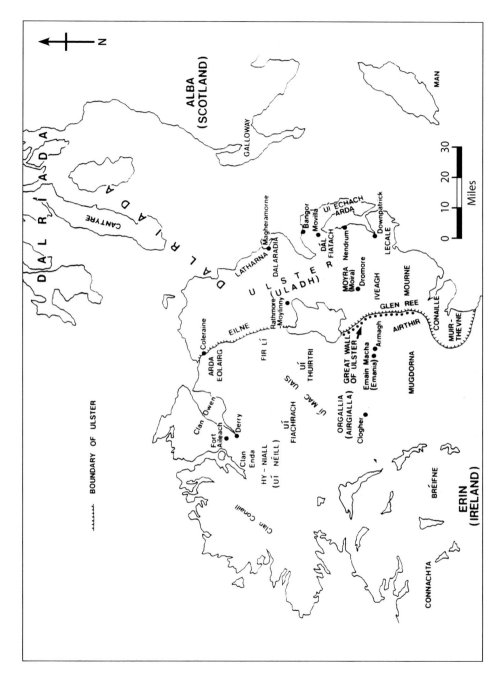

4. Ulster in the seventh century

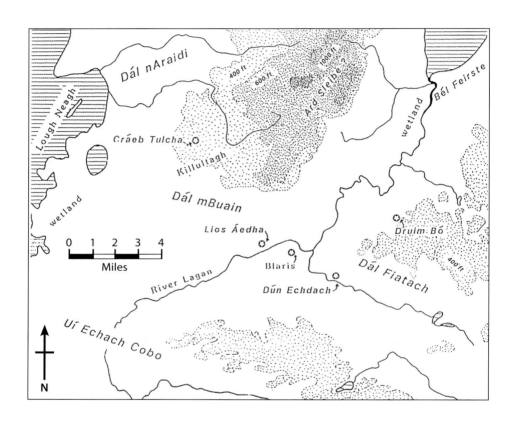

5. Cráeb Tulcha (Crew Hill)

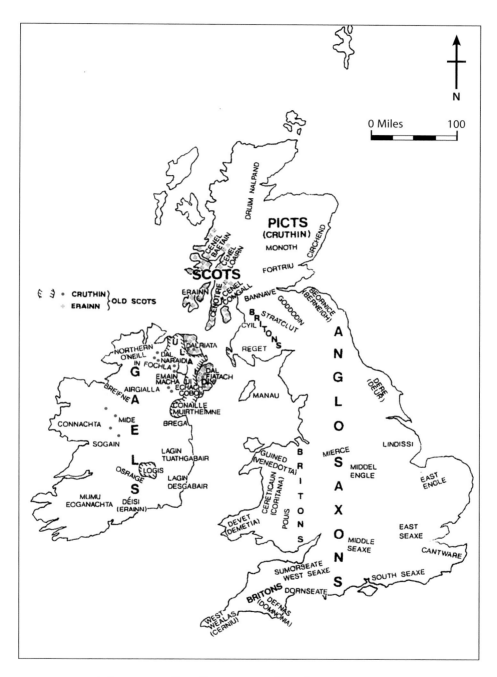

6. The British Isles in Early Christian Times

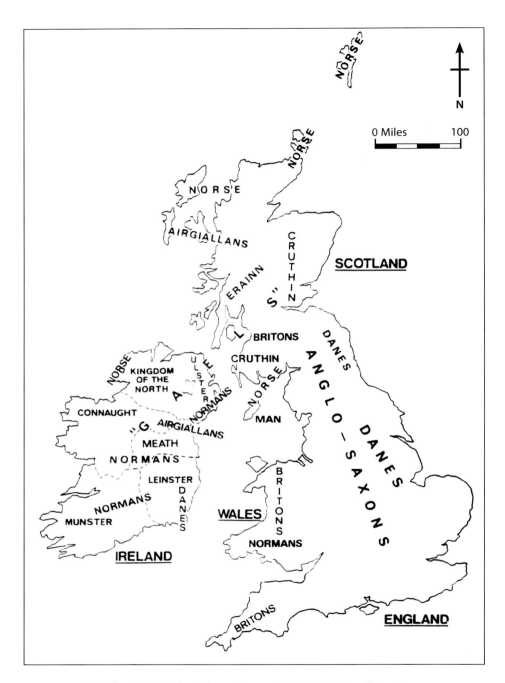

**7. The British Isles circa AD 1200 indicating
the 'Scandinavian' settlements**

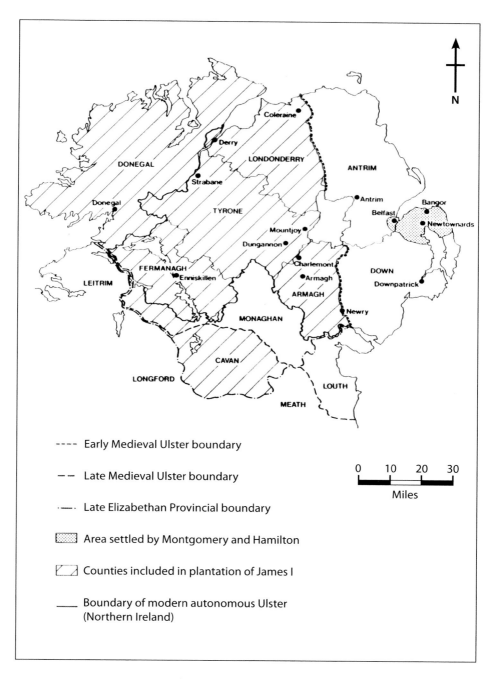

8. Seventeenth century settlements in Ulster

**9. The British Isles circa AD 1700 illustrating the
Civil Wars of the Three Kingdoms**

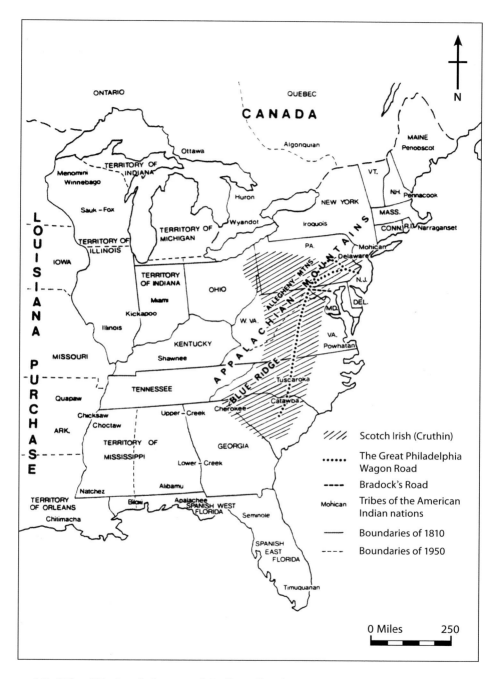

Scotch Irish (Cruthin)

The Great Philadelphia Wagon Road

Bradock's Road

Tribes of the American Indian nations

Boundaries of 1810

Boundaries of 1950

0 Miles   250

10. The United States (Columbia) in AD 1810 indicating the extent of Ulster settlement in the eighteenth century

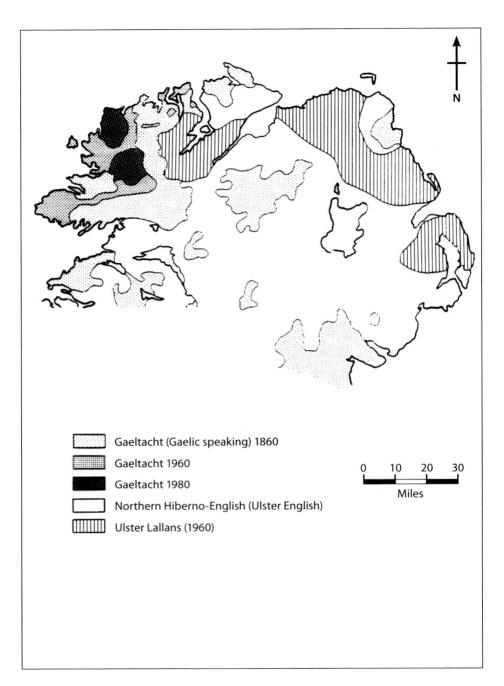

Gaeltacht (Gaelic speaking) 1860

Gaeltacht 1960

Gaeltacht 1980

Northern Hiberno-English (Ulster English)

Ulster Lallans (1960)

N

0   10   20   30
Miles

11. The language of Ulster

SELECT BIBLIOGRAPHY

Adamnan, *Life of Columba*, edited from Reeve's text by JT Fowler, Oxford University Press, Oxford, 1894.

An Archaeological Survey of County Down, Her Majesty's Stationery Office, Belfast, 1966.

Atkinson, ED, *Dromore, an Ulster Diocese*, W Tempest, Dundalgan Press, Dundalk, 1925.

Barber, Richard, *The Figure of Arthur*, Longman, London, 1972.

Beckett, JC, *The Making of Modern Ireland 1603–1923*, Faber and Faber, London, 1966.

Bede, *A History of the English Church and People*, Shirley-Price, Leo, trans, Penguin Books, London, 1955.

Bethan, Sir W, *The Gael and Cymbri* or *History of the Irish Scotti, Britons and Gaels*, Dublin, 1834.

Bromwich, R, *The Welsh Triads (Trioedd Ynys Prydain)*, Cardiff, 1961.

Brooke, Daphne, *Wild Men and Holy Places: St Ninian and the Medieval Realm of Galloway*, Canongate Books, Edinburgh, 1995.

Byrne, Francis, J, *Irish Kings and High-Kings*, Batsford Ltd, London, 1973.

Colles, Ramsey, *The History of Ulster*, Gresham Publishing Co Ltd, 1919.

Cruden, Stewart, *The Early Christian and Pictish Monuments of Scotland*, Her Majesty's Stationery Office, Edinburgh, 1964.

Davies, Oliver, 'A summary of the Archaeology of Ulster', *Ulster Journal of Archaeology*, 3rd Series, Vol XI, 1948.

Dick, Rev CH, *Highways and Byways in Galloway and Carrick*, Macmillan & Co, London, 1927.

Flanagan, LNW, *Ulster*, Regional Archaeologies Series, Heinemann Educational Books Ltd, London, 1970.

Flower, Robin, *The Irish Tradition*, Oxford University Press, Oxford, 1947.

Gallico, Paul, *The Steadfast Man, A Life of St Patrick*, Michael Joseph Ltd, London, 1958.

Hayward, Richard, *In Praise of Ulster*, illustrated by Humbert Craig, J, (first published) Arthur Barker of London, London, 1938.

Hayward, Richard, *Ulster and the City of Belfast* and *Border Foray*, Arthur Barker, London, illustrated by Raymond Piper, 1950 and 1957.

Healy, J, *Ireland's Ancient Schools and Scholars*, Sealy, Bryers & Walker, Dublin, 1902.

Henderson, Isabel, *The Picts*, and Powell, TGE, *The Celts*, Ancient Peoples and Places Series, Thames and Hudson Ltd, London, 1967.

Hennessy, William M, ed and trans, *The Annals of Ulster*, Vol 1, AD 431–1056, Her Majesty's Stationery Office, Dublin, 1887.

Hill, Peter, *Whithorn and St Ninian*, The Whithorn Trust, Sutton Publishing, Stroud, 1997.

Hutchinson, Wesley, *Espaces de l'imaginaire unionist nord-irlandais*, Presses Universitaires de Caen, France, 1999.

Jackson, Kenneth H, trans, *The Gododdin of Aneirin*, Edinburgh University Press, Edinburgh, 1969.

Jones, Gwyn, and Jones, Thomas, trans, *The Mabinogion*, Everyman's Library, London, 1949.

Lacey, Brian, *Cenél Conaill and the Kingdoms of Donegal AD 500–800*, Four Courts Press, Dublin and Portland Oregon, USA, 2006.

Lawlor, HC, *The Monastery of St Mochaoi of Nendrum*, Belfast Natural History and Philosophical Society, Belfast, 1925.

Lett, Rev HW, 'The Great Wall of Ulidia', in *Ulster Journal of Archaeology*, 2nd Series, Vol III, No I, 1897.

Leyburn, James G, *The Scotch-Irish*, Chapel Hill, The University of North Carolina Press, 1962.

Macalister, RAS, ed and trans, *Lebor Gabála Erenn*, Parts I–V Irish Texts Society, Dublin, completed 1956.

Mackenzie, WC, Gardiner, Alexander, *The Races of Ireland and Scotland*, Paisley, Scotland, 1949.

MacLysaght, E, *The Surnames of Ireland*, Irish University Press, Shannon, Ireland, 1969.

MacNeill, Eoin, 'The Pretanic Background in Britain and Ireland', *Journal of the Royal Society of Antiquaries of Ireland*, 1933, Vol LXIII, Part 1.

MacQueen, John, *Welsh and Gaelic in Galloway*, Transactions and Journal of Proceedings, Dumfriesshire and Galloway Natural History and Antiquarian Society, 1955.

Menzies, G, ed, *Who are the Scots?* BBC, London, 1971.

Moody, TW, and Martin, FX, eds, *The Course of Irish History*, Mercier Press, Cork, 1967.

Mullin, TH, and Mullan, JE, *The Ulster Clans*, Belfast, 1966.

O'Connor, Tom, *Hand of History, Burden of Pseudo History*, Trafford Publishing, Victoria BC, Canada and Oxford, United Kingdom, 2005.

O'Rahilly, Thomas, F, *Early Irish History and Mythology*, Dublin Institute for Advanced Studies, Dublin, 1964.

Pender, Seamus, MA, 'The Fir Domnann', *Journal of the Royal Society of Antiquaries of Ireland*, 1933, Vol LXIII, Part 1.

Pooler, LA, *A Short History of the Church of Ireland*, Olley & Co, Belfast, 1890.

Powell, TGE, 'Barbarian Europe, from the first farmers to the Celts', from *Dawn of Civilisation*, Sunday Times Publications, London, 1961.

Robertson, John F, *The Story of Galloway*, Outram and Co Ltd, Castle Douglas, Scotland, 1963.

Scott, Archibald B, *The Pictish Nation, its people and its Church*, TN Foulis of Edinburgh and London, Boston, Australasia, Cape Colony and Toronto, September 1918.

Smout, TC, *A History of the Scottish People 1560–1830*, William Collins, Glasgow, 1969.

Stone, Brian, trans, *Sir Gawain and the Green Knight*, Penguin Classics, London, 1959.

Stokes, George, *Ireland and the Celtic Church*, London, 1907.

Táin Bó Cúailnge from the Book of Leinster, O'Rahilly, Cecile, ed, Dublin Institute for Advanced Studies, Dublin, 1970.

'The Dal Fiatch', Dobbs, Margaret E, *Ulster Journal of Archaeology*, 3rd Series, Vol VIII, 1945.

The Imperial Gazetter of Scotland, Edinburgh.

The Prophet Ezekiel in *The Holy Bible*.

Thomas, Sir Charles, *Britain and Ireland in Early Christian Times AD 400–800*, Thomas & Hudson Ltd, London, 1971.

Walmsley, Thomas, Mogey, John M, and Gamble, David P, 'The Peoples of Northern Ireland: An Anthropometric Survey', *Ulster Journal of Archaeology*, 3rd Series, Volume IX, 1946.

Watson, WJ, *The Celts (British and Gael) in Dumfriesshire and Galloway*, Transactions of the Dumfriesshire and Galloway Natural History and Antiquarian Society.

Woodburn, James Barkley, *The Ulster Scot*, London, 1914.

Wright, Thomas, *The Celt, the Roman and the Saxon*, Hall Virtue & Co, 1852 – including works of Julius Caesar, Tacitus and Ammianus Marcellinus.

INDEX

WORKS BY DR IAN ADAMSON OBE

Books

The Cruthin: The Ancient Kindred, 1st edn Newtownards, Nosmada Books 1974; 2nd edn Bangor, Donard Publishing Co, 1978; 3rd edn Bangor, Pretani Press 1986; 5th imp 1995, ISBN 0-9503461-0-1

Bangor, Light of the world, 1st edn Bangor, Fairview Press, 1979; 2nd edn Belfast, Pretani Press, 1987, ISBN 0-948868-06-6

The Battle of Moira, [ed] *Sir Samuel Ferguson*, Congal, Newtownards, Nosmada Books, 1980.

The Identity of Ulster: The Land, the Language and the People,
1st edn Belfast, Pretani Press, 1982; 2nd edn 1987; 5th imp 1995,
ISBN 0-948868-04-X

The Ulster People: Ancient, Medieval and Modern, Bangor, Pretani Press, 1991, ISBN 0-948868-13-9

1690: William and the Boyne, Newtownards, Pretani Press, 1995,
ISBN 0-948868-20-1

Dalaradia, Kingdom of the Cruthin, Belfast, Pretani Press, 1998,
HB ISBN 0-948868-26-0 PB ISBN 0-948868-25-2

Bombs on Belfast: The Blitz 1941, Newtownards, Colourpoint Books in association with *Belfast Telegraph,* 2011; First published Belfast, Pretani Press, 1984, ISBN 978-1-906578-91-6